I0414880

Not Once, Not Twice But Three Times

A Mother's Story in Being an Advocate in Dealing with Children's Hidden Disabilities and 504 Plans

By

Sahron Ollie

© 2002 by Sahron Ollie. All rights reserved.

No part of this book may be reproduced, stored in a retrieval system, or transmitted by any means, electronic, mechanical, photocopying, recording, or otherwise, without written permission from the author.

ISBN: 0-7596-8911-3

This book is printed on acid free paper.

1stBooks – rev. 03/12/02

Table of Contents

Introduction

I have been an elementary teacher for twenty-four years and the mother of three children with special needs. When I was younger, I was very naive and thought that the best interest of the child would always be considered. I learned my knowledge of 504 Plans and hidden disabilities through the hard way. Eventually, I became someone more aggressive and was known as the 'B' mom. Often, I have entered a room full of professionals geared toward intimidating me. The usual method has been to use technical language that a parent is too embarrassed to ask for more clarification. Nevertheless, when these situations have another professional in the hanger, those methods do not work. Sometimes the reply of being one of them, insinuates one's security of a teaching position and the intended victim becomes nervous. If I had to do it again, I would never have lived in the same district where I taught at.

From my personal experiences, as well being a teacher, I am aware of students with hidden disabilities. Although, my profession does not allow me to state what I know and what I have learned, otherwise, I could be held liable. Often, I wish I could have said something to a parent, even if the child were not a student of mine. Many students would qualify for the 504 Plan. Sometimes, they are misplaced into a special education program. Two of my three children could have been placed that way, but their needs would not have been met.

Ultimately, I have become a better teacher. I use various strategies in helping all of my students succeed. It is just a simple matter of respecting the child and knowing the key to that child's success. Too often I have witnessed teachers wanting to mold the child to their way of instructing, instead of providing reasonable accommodations for that child. In certain situations, the only way of attempting to insure that a child is given appropriate instruction is by implementing the 504 Plan.

The 504 Plan is an individual educational plan written to fit that specific child. The child must have a disability and cannot qualify for special education. A medical doctor must diagnose this disability. The doctor needs to write a letter of diagnosis and hopefully will include suggestions for classroom accommodations. In my situation, when they diagnosed my first child with a disability, I did not know that I needed a letter from a doctor. I did not realize the importance of having a letter and what it would legally entail. I would simply approach the teachers and state my child's disability. They diagnosed Lisa, my oldest offspring, with CAPD (central auditory processing disorder) in the sixth grade. I only asked for preferential seating and that homework should not be given orally, since she always managed to do the wrong homework. Obtaining a simple courtesy, for my child's disability, was impossible.

So, when did I learn about 504 Plans? It did not come from a doctor, organization or co-worker. It came from a new principal at Lisa's middle school. She introduced me to the 504 Plan. I learned that 504 Plans had been around for twenty years. It is just that no one wants to be held accountable for maintaining one, since it is considered a legal matter under the Department of Civil Rights.

My story is true and some events that take place might be shocking and unbelievable. I have withheld the actual names of people, places and events to protect my family's privacy. From my experience and personal commitment in helping others, I decided to share my story. Included in my story, will be copies of my children's 504 Plans and their medical letters of diagnosis. Anyone can become familiar with hidden disabilities and the importance of knowing the law, reading my true-life experience.

Chapter One

Unaware of CAPD
(Lisa's Birth and Preschool Years)

Our little dark cloud was born on September 10, 1982. She was two weeks late and I had twenty-four hours of hard labor. I had died and an emergency C-section brought Lisa into this world. When she took her first breath, she kept on crying. She spent more time crying than sleeping. The nurses kept bringing her back for a feeding. They thought that she was hungry. Lisa weighed nine pounds and five ounces at birth. Since she was a large baby, they had assumed she was terribly hungry. Later, they had a volunteer rock Lisa to sleep and they quickly nicknamed her, 'the rocking chair baby.' When I took my long walks down the hall to see her, she was seldom on display. The volunteer was rocking her.

Five days later, I took Lisa home to my parents' house. My husband was attending Army boot camp for the National Guard. It was one way in which he could receive money to go to college. He had plans of graduating in the field of geology. If I did not have my parents, I do not know what I would have done. I required personal care for my health and my baby daughter kept on crying. She cried twenty hours per day and slept a mere four hours. When I had enough strength, I took her to a pediatrician. They informed me that she had severe colic, but they did not give me any medication for her. The only relief that Lisa received was listening to peaceful music, as I rocked her on her stomach. Eventually, I returned to my teaching position and my mother agreed to take care of Lisa. I was eternally grateful.

When I moved out of my parents' house, I obtained a small apartment close to my work place. The day that Ron returned home from boot camp and held his little girl, was the day that

Lisa stopped crying so often. Ron obtained two part-time jobs, while attending college. I had assumed that Lisa's crying was due to severe colic, since I had read that colicky babies had the problem for the first three months of their life. They are supposed to be very intelligent babies. Finally, we thought the problem of Lisa's crying had ended. When she began her long periods of crying again, I had assumed that it was from teething. I would rock her and sometimes I took her for a drive in the car. The sound of the motor would lure her to sleep.

Lisa turned out to be quite intelligent. She began crawling at four months of age. Lisa spoke in phrases at eight months. Of course, the latter would be difficult to prove, especially when they misdiagnosed her later. Lisa would use a high-pitched voice and say phrases like, 'come back here' and 'I love daddy.' Two months later, she was not doing any talking and her fits of crying became worse. I took off from work and took her to an ear specialist. They examined her and informed me that nothing was wrong with her. The doctor had inferred that when a child is learning to walk, she might not be interested in talking. I felt that he did not believe me about her talking, since it was highly unlikely that she would be for her age. Less than a week later, she developed a high fever of 105 degrees and had diarrhea. We rushed her to a nearby hospital. The hospital had us sponge bathe her to get the fever down and they gave her some Tylenol. Lisa had a severe ear infection and an appointment was arranged to take her to a child's ear specialist.

Apparently, Lisa had this infection for quite sometime. Noticing it by a pediatrician or another doctor was not easy, since a baby's auditory channel is quite small. The other ear specialist should have noticed it! The fluid behind her eardrums had to be drained. I quickly learned the three types of fluid that can cause ear infections. Lisa's was the hardest to detect, since it is way back in the ear.

I will never forget the day that Lisa was sitting on the bed heading for surgery. They had her sit in the middle and they would strap her down later. They did not allow us to watch the surgery, since they told us to sit in the waiting room. They gave Lisa a happy pill to relax her and then they would put her to sleep for the surgery. Lisa would have the surgical implants in her ears, until the doctor felt they were ready for removal. Presently, Lisa had only 40 percent of her hearing. She could hear the same as someone listening underwater. Talking with her was very difficult. I read to her, even though, I was not sure exactly what she was hearing. I felt that perhaps she could feel the vibrations. She loved looking at the pictures and would make comparisons by pointing to the various similarities. I played games with her, such as blocks and puzzles. We went to the park often, and she loved being on the swings. It was here that I had no choice but to listen to other parents' brag about how smart their child was. "Well, Billy knows one hundred words" and "Suzie has learned her ABC's." People would try to converse with Lisa and she could not acknowledge them.

Eventually, my mother became tired of watching Lisa and I had to place her in a preschool. One was near our apartment. At that time, Lisa was two and a half years old and had her tubes surgically removed. It would take time for the small holes in her eardrums to heal. Lisa was not talking. She would usually point to things when she wanted something. It was amazing that she was potty-trained. She would pat her behind to tell me when she needed to go to the bathroom.

Well, I did not know much about preschools or daycare centers. I thought she would be better off there, than at a private home. The preschool I had selected, seemed to be the ideal place. The director had a college degree in education and seemed attentive in what I had to say about Lisa. I informed the school about Lisa's condition. The school appeared to offer a nurturing environment and appeared well organized. Parents would drop their children off in the waiting area and at the end of the day, children were packed up and ready to go home. Parents did not have to wait.

3

One day my mother and I went to pick up Lisa. We found her lying in a fetal position, moaning to herself. Her hair was combed differently, than the way it had been that morning. Lisa was very withdrawn. I questioned her teacher. The teacher admitted giving Lisa two swats on the behind in the bathroom, because she refused to take a nap. Since they did not allow spanking, I made an issue about it in front of the other parents. We left with Lisa and headed to the shopping mall. Usually, whenever I go shopping, I have Lisa visit the restroom facilities. When Lisa saw the bathroom, she freaked out. She cried like there was no tomorrow. Huge tears fell from her eyes. I was lucky that my mother was there. She quickly made the assumption that they had dunked Lisa in water. That type of punishment would leave no marks. Since Lisa could not talk, we would never know for sure. My mother volunteered to watch Lisa, until we could make other arrangements. They dismissed Lisa's teacher from her job and for several weeks I received harassing phone calls. It took several months before Lisa could go into any bathroom. I bought a potty-horse and had to place it a few feet from the bathroom door. Each day I moved it closer to the bathroom. When finally it was in the bathroom, it was a matter of getting her to move from the potty-horse to the toilet seat. I kept a jar of jellybeans by the toilet seat. I would allow Lisa to reach in the jar and pull some out, if she sat on the seat. Eventually, her hunger for the jellybeans overcame her fear.

A day came when my mother was tired of her small apartment and wanted to move back home. I needed her to continue watching Lisa. So, I agreed to live back home and Ron (my husband) would share an apartment with my middle brother, Keith. Ron was still attending college and only had a moped to ride. Lisa and I would see him on the weekends. Again my mother became tired of watching Lisa and so I had to find another daycare. I found a preschool, near my place of employment, that was run by nuns. I thought that a place with a religious atmosphere would be good for Lisa.

A week after Lisa started this preschool, one of the nuns requested an appointment with me. She felt that something was terribly wrong with my child. According to her, Lisa was slow and obviously showed signs of being mentally-handicapped. Lisa needed to be placed in a special program. I explained Lisa's past and I felt that Lisa needed a chance to catch up. Nevertheless, the nun was very persistent on claiming that the tests showed that Lisa's IQ range was between sixty and seventy. I felt that this preschool could not help Lisa, since they had already labeled her. I kept Lisa in there for a few more weeks and then my mother began watching her again.

It was very difficult staying with my parents. Although, they loved Lisa and me, it was not easy for any of us. Finally, came the time I had to move out. Ron decided to drop out of college and just get a regular full-time job, instead of the part-time job he had. It would have to be a job that would not interfere with the Army National Guard. We found a small duplex near where I worked. Ron increased his hours as a security officer to full-time employment.

We were able to pay for a sitter for a few months, until Allen was born. Later, the sitter needed more money to watch both children and we did not have it. Luckily, Ron could get evening work and sometimes watch the children during the day. A church nearby offered childcare services and they were willing to work with us. So, Lisa and Allen went there. Financially, we were hurting. The chance for my husband to have a career was nonexistent. We lived in a rural area that had little opportunity. Our life with two children was very dismal. So, after careful consideration, Ron joined the Navy. We were very fortunate that they were willing to take us, since we had two children. When Ron left for boot camp, my mom stayed with us. She took care of Allen, while Lisa began attending a brand-new preschool. Every day when I went to pick her up, she was always sitting on the bench. Lisa was speaking a few words, but still had a limited vocabulary. So, I never really knew the truth behind all of this.

Apparently, she was always pushing the children off the swings and would not wait her turn. It was almost impossible to explain to anyone the circumstances regarding Lisa and that there was not a quick fix for helping her. My professional instinct was to put her back a year. She needed to socialize with children that were a year younger, so she could have a chance to catch up. However, the preschool refused my request.

One day I heard about a special research program that my alma mater sponsored. A team of five educators were testing children for a special program. They were looking for children that were very intelligent, but because of learning disabilities would have potential trouble in school. Well, that sounded like the perfect program for Lisa. The day I went, I saw at least one hundred children there. A great deal of paperwork had to be filled out. While I was working on it, they gave Lisa different activities to do. She was very active compared with the other children. Lisa constantly touched things and was a bit grabby. I kept wondering when they were going to pull her from the others and tell me to take her home. The team was very patient and wasn't bothered by Lisa's restlessness. They gave a final activity to do with puzzles that required instant memorization. After that activity, they politely asked everyone to leave, but they told me to stay. I thought this was strange.

Two of the researchers met with me and informed me that Lisa was the type of child that would fit into their program. None of the other children had passed the high intellectual test to do with puzzles. They asked me to take Lisa to their audiology department and have her hearing tested there, and do a few other tests to decide her IQ. Through their extensive testing, they informed me that Lisa had a high to moderate hearing frequency loss, but had the possibility of having a high IQ. The audiologist informed me that it would take time, before Lisa would catch up with her age group on communication skills. I gladly signed Lisa up with their special program. However, it was not meant for her to attend. Ron had arranged for us to live in the state where he received his military training.

In Illinois, I worked as a childcare provider in our apartment. I took care of Lisa and Allen, along with some other children. Paying the bills was very difficult, because my clients were sometimes late in paying me. Therefore, I became involved with the school system and was given an assistant teaching job, until I received my teaching license from the state. It took a year to obtain that license! I had great difficulty in keeping a sitter. I went through three sitters in a two-week period. Their reasons were all different. Finally, sitter number four worked out for me. She took great care of my two children. I always made sure that I promptly paid her, because I did not want to lose her. During that time, I was still concerned about Lisa's hearing and speaking and so I took her to an audiologist on the base. He found nothing wrong with her hearing. Even though, he looked over the paperwork that had been done previously. He told me that the military only checked for normal speaking frequency. Lisa showed that she did not have any difficulty in those areas. She could handle regular school when the time came. Naturally, none of it made any sense. It did not matter, since we would be leaving to go to another state. Ron would be receiving further training in his military career.

In January 1987, we moved. I was fortunate to obtain a permanent substitute position for the remainder of the school year. I found a babysitter, at least for a short time. The sitter had trouble with Lisa, but not with Allen. One day when I came to pick them up, the sitter had Lisa pinned to the floor, with a friend of hers watching. I told her to get off Lisa and I was prepared to do whatever it took to get her off! She told me that Lisa had thrown the toys in the backyard over the fence. A dog next door had chewed on the toys and ruined them. She felt she would have to raise the babysitting fee from sixty-five dollars to ninety dollars. I told her that I would not pay it and that she had no business restraining my daughter. I told her that I would make other arrangements for child care services. At this time, Lisa was speaking in phrases and was able to tell me what had happened at the sitter's home, along with the help from Allen. Allen had excellent speaking skills for his age. Both of them, explained that the sitter's two daughters did not allow them to play with their toys. So, Lisa threw the toys over the fence.

A preschool was near our apartment. The preschool took both children, even though, Allen was not two years old. He would be in a few weeks. So, they asked me to remain quiet about the issue. The child care fee was the same, as the fee for the sitter had been. I was skeptical about their facility, but was more relieved to know that I could pick up my children anytime I wanted. I could walk into their classrooms' unannounced. Lisa had trouble with some children and I had met with the director and explained about Lisa's late development in communication skills and her hearing problem. The facility was lenient with Lisa, but Lisa kept getting into trouble. If she did not get her favorite colored cereal bowl, she would throw the bowl on the floor. She would take other children's bowls and do the same thing. She took pictures off the walls and would throw them on the floor, too. I sat with her and talked to her face to face. Lisa was told that if she did that again, she would get a spanking. She never did that particular crime again.

Later, I learned about a program for special needs children, known as a 'generic kindergarten program.' They informed me that once when a parent signs papers for any state program, that child could not be taken out of the program. I learned that a private source would be the best method to obtain information about your child, so that it could be kept confidential. Still, I wanted Lisa in that program. At times, I did not think she was hearing me and her vocabulary could use some additional help. In fact, Allen could speak better than her! So, I arranged to have her tested at the facility. They tested her knowledge of the alphabet, her color words, if she could climb stairs, fasten and unfasten buttons and if she could tie her shoes. During Lisa's testing, I was supposed to fill out some paperwork. Instead, I watched Lisa being tested and was surprised at what she could do. They allowed me to take the paperwork home to complete. The tester asked me to call Monday and they would give me the results. Over the weekend, I decided to attend a nearby church. A friend of mine had invited me. My friend knew of Lisa's disability and showed me another hearing-impaired child sitting a few pews up. This little girl was nine years old and would finally begin first grade. She had attended the generic kindergarten program for three years. As I watched the little girl, I came to a swift decision. Maybe, this generic kindergarten program was not the best solution for Lisa's needs. When I began to fill out the paperwork, I saw that it mentioned the use of diapers. When I called that Monday, they told me that Lisa had failed the test and that she was a slow learner. I quickly asked about the diaper business. Apparently, all the special needs' children were placed in the same room and that they would pull her out to receive help in speech. Lisa would be in the program, until they felt that she was ready to go to first grade. Well, again, this was not the program for Lisa. I knew that Lisa had passed most of her tests. Something was terribly wrong with this arrangement. I kept Lisa at the preschool and entered her into their kindergarten program. Persuading the facility to keep her in the same classroom for another year, was pointless. They definitely wanted her passed on to the next program. Eventually, I would be given the opportunity to keep Lisa back one year and give her the necessary time to catch up. Later, I learned that the 'generic kindergarten program' was playing the numbers game. In order, to keep the number of teachers and assistants at their facility, depended upon the number of students. They had tried simply to use Lisa to fill their required statistics.

My youngest child was born on August 21, 1987. Kim was an entirely different baby than Lisa had been. She was like a ray of sunshine. Lisa was not an affectionate child when she was younger, but Kim was. As Lisa grew older, she became more affectionate. Lisa fell in love with Kim. She became a little mother. Surprisingly, she never showed this side of herself to Allen. It might have been the timing. Lisa made sure that Kim was fed and looked after. As the years progressed, she took up for her little sister several times. Occasionally, she would take up for Allen, too.

For the 1987-88 school year, I received a contract and began teaching second grade at another school. My previous principal had given me a contract at her school, but I was late in beginning the school year, due to Kim's birth. Luckily, I received a position closer to where I lived. Lisa began kindergarten at the preschool and Allen remained in the two-year-old program. I was very lucky in finding a sitter for Kim. The sitter was dependable and watched Kim for more than a year.

Well, Lisa's year in kindergarten was not a good experience for her. Lisa's teacher had a difficult time with her. I attended several meetings about Lisa's defiant behavior. Lisa would do things differently than the other children. One day I saw a group display of colored turkeys. One was colored purple. Naturally, I knew that it just had to be Lisa's. Another time, when I went to pick up Lisa and Allen, they asked me to step into the director's office. It turned out that Lisa had kicked him in the leg. She had been wearing a sheet over her head, pretending to be a ghost. She had been scaring the other children and causing such a commotion that the teacher had to send for the director. I thought for sure that they would expel her from the school. Well, they did not! Again Lisa and I had a private conversation and Lisa never did it again.

One day I came early to pick up Lisa and Allen. Lisa was in the hallway and I witnessed her getting a spanking from an assistant. I asked what the problem was. I never got a reasonable answer. They dismissed the assistant. I never knew how long this had been going on. I could not get a straight answer out of Lisa. Maybe, that was why Lisa was so defiant. Looking back at her personal kindergarten pictures and her classroom picture, I never saw her smile. On her face was a look of confusion and sadness. Even though, Lisa's earlier years lacked stability, her problem with socializing and learning, would turn out to be a physical disability and not a psychological one.

Chapter Two

CAPD is a Misunderstood Disability...
(Lisa's Elementary Years)

When Lisa turned six years old, she began first grade at the school at which I taught. I obtained an out-of-district permit for her, since my husband was in the military and he was not able to help with child care. At the time, it was a good idea for her to come with me. I had misgivings about Lisa attending first grade. I felt that she was not socially ready. For the first two weeks, Lisa sat by herself at lunch. Her shoulders were slumping and she was withdrawn. I had several conferences with her teacher and it was decided that Lisa would go back to kindergarten. Thank goodness! At the school, they gave Lisa speech therapy three times a week. Lisa began to make friends and her vocabulary began to increase. I should have been satisfied with those results, but I was not. Deep down inside, I knew that something was still wrong with Lisa. Sometimes, she would not respond to someone talking to her. She acted as if she were antisocial. The following year I had the school check her hearing. It was strange that Lisa would keep raising her hand, after the machine was turned off. The school audiologist did not have an answer to why Lisa was doing that. Her first grade teacher, began to notice that Lisa did better on her tests, if she sat in front of the room. She mentioned a possible hearing problem. I gradually learned that the staff at my school was supportive of Lisa and that was because I worked there. For the six years that Lisa attended elementary school, I felt that she did receive a decent education. The teachers would place her in front of the classroom, but they really did not have to. I did not have a scrap of evidence to support the issue of her hearing. Sometimes, Lisa was on the honor roll. Frequently, she did the wrong homework assignment, but was allowed to redo it. These homework assignments were given orally at the end of the day. She had trouble on her spelling tests, because she could not quite distinguish certain sounds. Lisa received two years of speech therapy and was dismissed from the program.

One of the most important things that bothered me about Lisa was her consistent inability to respond, when someone spoke to her. Speaking directly in front of her, she would respond. However, speaking to her from the side or behind her, she seldom responded. I would have to tell her that so and so just spoke to her. Lisa would respond by saying, 'I know, I just did not want to say anything.' This would happen quite frequently.

Lisa was not much help around the house, except taking care of Kim. It was impossible to give her more than one direction at a time. Lisa could never handle a multiple set of directions. Asking her to repeat the directions, did not work. She still could not follow through.

Lisa's fifth grade year was rough. I guess it was because of the hormonal growth that children go through. She would run into my classroom, whenever a personal problem existed between her and her peers. Doing this was easy for her, since the restroom was near my classroom. Eventually, her teacher caught wind of it and she did not like it. I could not blame her. Lisa had to handle personal problems on her own.

I remembered one incident prompted by another parent. One morning I was downstairs doing hall duty. Lisa walked in the morning, from the babysitter's house to school, with the other neighborhood children. I wanted Lisa to fill part of the school and so I dropped her off in the mornings at Mrs. Lee's house. Another child approached Lisa, while the child's mother stood watching. The child boldly kicked Lisa in the leg. I was standing nearby, but not close enough. Someone else intervened and told the parent whose daughter that was and I was right over there. As I walked toward the scene, the parent took off. The young person, who had kicked Lisa, headed off toward the cafeteria for breakfast. I asked Lisa about the situation and she informed me about a conflict that had occurred on a previous day. Then, I could not chase after the child or do any further investigating, since I had to complete my hall duty. When the bell rang, I went directly to Lisa's classroom teacher and told her of the problem. I felt that it would be taken care of. As the students were lining up to go into their classrooms, I saw the girl get out of line and kick Lisa again. Well, Lisa did the same thing. My aggressive tigress had no intention of standing like a tree. Soon, the problem was resolved. Other situations like this occurred, throughout her fifth grade year.

Lisa began taking viola lessons in the fifth grade. It was something that she became proficient in. In fact, she made the accomplishment of being selected for the All-City Fifth-Grade Orchestra. Lisa stayed with the viola through middle school and high school.

Remembering all the details concerning Lisa has been hard. Allen was having some problems and then I had Kim. My husband was gone quite a bit, due to being on a ship. So, I had to handle the problems that came up. Sometimes, I had to weigh what was more important. I do remember taking Lisa several times to different audiologists for testing. Lisa always passed the tests. I still had no substantial evidence, just my continual gut feeling that a problem still existed.

Throughout Lisa's elementary years, I helped Lisa to become involved in community service, and creative opportunities. I started a local child's entertainment group. We performed using the boom box and tapes. My younger brother and I had written some songs to use. He primarily did the vocals with a guitar accompaniment. He came several times to visit and during those times was when we recorded the songs. Lisa enjoyed singing with the group. We sung several times for the Lion's Club and the local McDonald's. We did a little sign language that added more artistic appeal to the group. During our rehearsals, Lisa made a few close friends. Our team met after school in the auditorium and the parents would help with picking up their children. We all became quite close. Once when Lisa entered middle school, I discontinued the program.

During those years, Lisa took art lessons, ballet lessons, swimming lessons, karate and piano at the nearby community centers, with my other two children. She was good at these creative avenues. At one time, I was hoping that she would become more involved in becoming a lifeguard. She was on a community swim team, but she did not pursue it. She learned what she needed from each of these activities and that was all. Lisa also got involved with the Girl Scouts, but it turned out to be too cliquish and we stopped going. One reason, was that I worked at a job that required more than a forty-hour week. Being a volunteer and to help out with the many activities that they expected, was just not possible for me.

The summer before Lisa entered sixth-grade, they accepted her at a special summer program for potentially gifted academic students. At first, Lisa did not pass the interview, because she could not hear the questions given by the interviewer. I thought it was unusual that the interview was a short one. As we left the building and headed for the car, I asked Lisa about the interview. 'I did not do very well,' she murmured. 'Why', I questioned. 'Because I could not understand what she was saying,' she murmured back. Well, I had to take the initiative. We hurried back to the building and I spoke with the person in charge. I explained the situation and Lisa received a different interviewer. I kept on identifying Lisa with a hearing problem, when I knew I had no real evidence. I think they accepted Lisa into the program, because they wanted a special needs' student. This would politically help their program. A total of only twenty slots were available and two hundred students apply. Later, their program was more known for ethnic students. Lisa had good ITBS test scores in the fourth and fifth grade. In fact, they asked her to attend the public school's summer enrichment program, funded by the state. Lisa scores were good in science and social studies. Her reading and math scores were average, except Spelling. Spelling was really low! Lisa loved attending this program. A bus came nearby and picked her up. She did not mind doing the homework activities. During her sixth-grade year, Lisa attended all the special opportunities that this program provided.

I met with Lisa's sixth-grade cluster teachers and explained to them about Lisa's hearing problem. Nevertheless, as mentioned earlier, I did not have any real proof. Although, I had requested that Lisa sit in the front of the room, they did not respect my request. In fact, they did not do much to help Lisa. It was truly a very rough year. I received many phone calls that year on how Lisa was socializing. She was always crying and being picked on. Lisa kept doing the wrong homework assignments and it was reflected in her grades. I became angry and more determined to prove that Lisa had some kind of disability and needed certain accommodations!

I took Lisa again to an audiologist and had her tested. Of course, they remembered me! This was one of the places I had taken her to in the past. I had an instinct to write everything down that concerned me about Lisa, because I knew she would again pass this hearing test. When the audiologist met with me, I was adamant about my observations of Lisa. Yet, on this day, the young female audiologist, listened to me. She told me that Lisa might have CAPD (central auditory processing disorder). They could test Lisa at the local naval hospital, because they had the facilities for it.

It took time to get the appointment, but on November 30 of that school year, my husband took Lisa in for the test. It took several hours and Lisa did have CAPD. They would send the test results to us. We received the packet in the mail and I felt that they could not have been more precise. They also included suggestions for classroom accommodations. Soon after I received the packet, I made an appointment to meet with her cluster teachers. Meeting with her teachers was a pure waste of time. The only help I received from them was directed to the office. I had to arrange to meet with the child study team. An office assistant made a copy of the packet and placed this information in Lisa's cumulative record.

When I met with them, most of them were cooperative. Attending this meeting, was the school psychologist, the social worker, the assistant principal, and Lisa's guidance counselor. Everyone seemed very helpful, except the guidance counselor. Mr. S., the counselor, was nothing but a problem. It began with him misplacing Lisa's paperwork from the naval hospital. Apparently, he could not find it in her cumulative record, which was in his possession. It was very annoying to have to deal with this. I grabbed the cumulative record from his hands and looked in it. It had to be in there! Well, it was! A complete disarray of papers was in her record. He had taken apart her packet and totally disorganized it. The rest of the team was completely aghast! It looked as if the meeting had to end, unless they could reorganize the papers. To their amazement and Mr. S's, I took out the original paperwork that I had in a folder. They made copies from the original and passed it out to the team. The team had not seen the report, only Mr. S. Great planning is what I called it! I thought that I would not have any more problems, well, I was wrong! When I began to read some suggested classroom accommodations, Mr. S. flared up! He told me that sending her to a school for the deaf would be better! At this point, the psychologist intervened and they decided that Lisa would receive a special IEP. She would not qualify for special education, since she was not failing and was not considered hearing-impaired. The team wrote some suggestions on headless carbon paper. The suggestions we needed were:

1. Verify that student has correctly written homework assignments for the next day.

2. Give the student only one direction at a time and face student when giving them.
3. Use visual aids
4. Provide vocabulary words in advance

Copies consisted of these suggestions and placed in the teachers' mailboxes. Nevertheless, it did not matter. The principal was retiring that year and nothing was enforced.

Lisa's first year at middle school was a traumatic experience for her. Lisa's grades severely suffered, during the last nine weeks. I was upset with four of her teachers, for not respecting the four classroom accommodations that were necessary for Lisa's success. To begin with, they accused Lisa of cheating on a communication skills' test. She was looking around the room and not keeping her eyes focused on the test. They apparently gave the oral directions for the test to the class, but not to Lisa's comprehension. Lisa had difficulty in her science class, because she could not hear the videos on which she was being tested. Again, Lisa would have to depend on her auditory skills and the use of visual aids was tossed out the window. Her social studies' teacher did not like Lisa staring at her, as she walked around the room talking. The same teacher had no respect for an individual's right of privacy, for she would share all individual test scores with the class. Lisa received a drop in her grade from her orchestra teacher, because she showed up late at the end-of-the year concert. She received the information orally and they did not write it down. Out of ignorance, these particular teachers would decide where Lisa would be placed for the rest of middle school. The stone had already been caste. Naturally, I was an outraged parent and should be. I had done my part on getting her properly diagnosed and thought that the school's IEP would be enough. I wrote a letter to the school system's administration and told them my concerns. Later, I received a letter in return and would meet with the new principal in the fall.

During that summer, Lisa was invited back to the private educational program, because she had kept up with her tutoring sessions. If they had heard about Lisa's low grades in two of her classes, they would have dropped her from the program. Lisa could not have below a 'C' in any subject. They did not find out, because they had not received her final report card. Their decision was based on the third nine weeks' grading period.

I deeply wanted Lisa to have a better school year, than what she had in sixth grade. I was very uneasy about the response of my letter and I wanted more ammunition about Lisa's disability. I had heard, from the grapevine, that the best doctor for audiology was Dr. S. He had the best reputation in the city! So, I took Lisa to see him. He did not have the facility to test Lisa for this condition, but went with the results from the naval hospital. Since then, I go every year to have Lisa's letter updated by him and she takes her usual hearing examination. As the years went by, his letters were vital in securing and maintaining Lisa's 504 Plan.

Chapter Three

Beginning to Understand CAPD and the 504 Plan

Before Lisa began seventh-grade, I decided to meet with the new principal, Ms. Y. I felt I had justified concerns and wanted to discuss them with her. I learned about the 504 Plan from Ms. Y. This new principal was knowledgeable in handling special needs' students, and knew a lot of legal jargon. She did receive an e-mail from one assistant superintendent, concerning Lisa and my letter. She did not want to wait for the child study team meeting, so she wrote a list of tentative suggestions for Lisa's new teachers to follow. The child study meeting would be necessary to attend, because they are the ones that initiate the 504 Plan. Gosh! I wondered why they did not do that last year. Anyway, the principal agreed on some suggestions that the naval hospital audiologists had made. One main suggestion that she should have agreed on was the use of a FM monitor. A FM monitor is a device that the auditory-impaired student wears and the teachers would wear a small mike. Using this equipment would deaden any outside noise and could have benefitted Lisa. She had told me that she did not want her teachers to be wearing a mike and that they did not have to. Well, I was ignorant. I bought what she had said. It turns out that I could have taken the matter to court. When I met with the child study team, the 504 IEP was set up for Lisa. The words, '504 Plan' is written at the top of this document, making it lawfully official. Some suggestions were to give Lisa priority seating, assign a study-buddy, write all homework assignments on the board, use visual stimuli in presenting material and give one oral direction at a time. Personal problems occurred, but nothing like the previous year.

During that summer, Lisa went to the state-supported enrichment program. A program designed for possible college candidates. Lisa qualified in this program, only from what she had done on state tests in fourth and fifth grade. I had mentioned a little of this program earlier. Lisa had spent two summers with the private summer enrichment program and was not invited back. Apparently, I had offended the director of the program. One day she had called me and expected an immediate return call. I was not able to call her until the next day. She was not available and I had to leave a message. Lisa had received an acceptance letter welcoming her back into the program. The director had wanted to interview all of the returning students and that was why she had initially called me. They sent out another letter, dismissing Lisa from the program. They dismissed her because she had made a 'D' in the first quarter and did not come for a tutoring session to bring it up. Lisa in the second grading quarter had brought that grade up to an 'A'. So, the remark about the grade was insignificant. I felt that it was for the best. Lisa was eager to begin the state-supported program, whereas, her 504 Plan would still be in effect.

The 504 Plan is protected under the Department of Civil Rights. A school system does not want to give out 504 Plans, since they are held liable for compensatory damages. Whereas, if a child is placed in special education, they do not handle it the same way. I learned that they assign a case manager for every 504 Plan. That person is the one who understands the student's disability and the one who will handle the parents' complaints. I thought it should be the guidance counselor, but instead the job can go to a classroom teacher.

During Lisa's eighth-grade year, her case manager was her homeroom and Social Studies teacher, Mr. C. Mr. C. was very close to retiring and did not understand about Lisa's disability. I made arrangements two weeks' in advance to meet with all of Lisa's teachers. Unfortunately, only Mr. C., the science teacher and the communication skills' teacher were present. The science teacher left early and so it ended being only two teachers. Having all of Lisa's teachers present, would have been more effective. As a classroom teacher, not attending this meeting was foolhardy. Mr. C. turned out to be a poor case manager. He did not set a good example for the other teachers, because he could not follow the 504 Plan. He took points off Lisa's graded work, if she did not follow the oral directions given. Furthermore, a problem developed with Lisa's Spanish teacher. As I became more experienced in dealing with 504 Plans, the resource teachers never realized that the 504 Plan included them. Ms.T., Lisa's Spanish teacher, never used any visual stimuli. Everything was done orally, including the testing. Without the use of visual stimuli, one may as well give Lisa a concrete block and ask her to take a swim. Ms.T. became harassing. I would receive phone messages from her and was asked to call her at school. Since, I also taught, getting the time to speak with her on the phone was difficult. We began to play phone tag. She left messages and I left messages. Finally, she sent me a letter in the mail along with some of Lisa's work. Lisa was failing Spanish I. My husband and I purchased a computer program and Lisa was learning the language. However, she would not pass Ms.T.'s class, due to the lack of using appropriate classroom accommodations. Previously, I had met with Lisa's guidance counselor and she had spoken with Ms.T. Ms. T. made it look as if she were trying. She worked with Lisa after school, but it was useless. Her oral methods were ineffective with Lisa. Soon after that, Lisa had been attacked in her Spanish class. Ms. T. was not in her class when it occurred. She had left and a substitute was not present. As I mentioned earlier, Lisa had trouble communicating with her peers. The tormentor sat behind Lisa and when Lisa did not respond to her taints, she pulled Lisa's hair. Lisa turned around and hit the young woman. The girl knocked Lisa out of her seat and literally dragged her by the hair on the floor. Someone went and got a security guard and they suspended both girls for one day. When Lisa returned to school, they asked me to go with her. I thought there would be a lecture from the assistant principal. Instead, they made it perfectly clear to me that both girls would not have this incident placed in their records. Could it have been that the attacker's mother was the PTA president? Maybe, it was because Lisa was on the 504 Plan or was it because a lawsuit could be pending, since the class was left unattended. I really did not care to pursue the incident. I simply wanted Lisa out of that classroom! Therefore, I sent a letter with the appropriate reasons for having Lisa taken out of the class, to Ms. Y. Lisa would be placed in a piano class and take Spanish I in high school next year. Apparently, someone did not want the incident to drop or perhaps it was another entire situation to do with Ms. T. During Lisa's last week in the Spanish class, a visitor came from the administrative office of the school system. According to Lisa, this person sat in Ms. T's desk and went through her lesson plan book and her grade book. When she was finished, she showed Ms. T. how to use visual stimuli to teach with. Lisa learned more in that one day, than she learned the entire time with this teacher.

An assistant superintendent asked me, the same as the one who received my letter about Lisa's sixth-grade experience, to come in and revise Lisa's 504 Plan. She supposedly had strategies to use with CAPD students. It was a crock! She had a handout used for ADD students. However, some of these accommodations were appropriate for Lisa. After this meeting, a dramatic difference in the instructional accommodations came from Lisa's other teachers. The teachers were extremely pleasant to her. Lisa became very uncomfortable, because they were too pleasant! She became unsure of her true ability and this affected her self-concept. At times, she thought that she did not deserve the grades she received. Lisa had a difficult time handling this new situation. It was very possible that these teachers were fabricating the issue, when it came to Lisa's grades. As a classroom teacher, it would be very simple to do. For example, one could spell the words for a child, while the child is composing it.

Lisa wanted her grades to be genuine. Her true ability was recognized in science, piano and strings. Lisa was not given top honors in her strings' class, since it was determined by her actual ability. In her piano class, she was excelling. Lisa had been taking piano lessons on Saturdays at the local community center. So, she was already skilled in this area. The class that she felt the most comfortable in was her science class. During the second semester, Lisa had been in the honors Earth Science class. She achieved this status all on her own, since her science teacher had already been using visual stimuli in her daily instruction. I noticed improvement in Lisa's writing and reading skills from being in this class. Then, Lisa became interested in only music and science.

That summer, Lisa took the first part of the Earth Science class, so she could take biology in high school. When Lisa graduated from middle school, she did receive a presidential seal for most improvement. Lisa had wanted the presidential seal for academic excellence and wanted to become a member of the Junior Honor Society. I felt she should be thrilled to have received the honor that she did. Lisa thought it was second-rate compared with what might have been. I thought it was a true recognition for her hard work and the disability she had to deal with on a daily basis.

Chapter Four

Moderate Cerebral Palsy Goes Undiagnosed
(Allen's Birth and Preschool Years)

Allen was born on April 11, 1985. I have considered him my Achilles' heel. I have been very vulnerable when it came to him. Allen was a planned C-section baby. Money was very tight for us. We did not believe in abortion and knew we would have to make some sacrifices and do the best we could. Ultimately, Ron had to drop out of college and enter the work force full-time. It was a difficult time for us. We hated living from paycheck to paycheck.

When Allen came into this world, he was the first baby born in a brand-new hospital. The local newspaper wanted to get a picture of him, but his nurses would not allow it. They were so protective over him. Later, five more babies entered the world and they were all females. Before Allen was born, they told me that he was lying in a diagonal position and would never have made it through the birth canal. It had been the same for Lisa. I never learned why this had occurred. That piece of information may have been important, since the same thing occurred again with my youngest child. Allen was a healthy eight pounds, eleven and half ounce baby. He appeared normal in every way. He was quiet most of the time. Allen had a little colic at night and his doctor prescribed colic medicine for the first three months. Sometimes, Allen was very active. When Allen was four months old, he was put in a walker. He went everywhere in that walker! He was so quick and agile. Before he was a year old, he was crawling and exploring. I had expected him to walk before he was a year old. Lisa had walked when she was eleven months old, and had not been as physically active. Allen was such a quick crawler, that I entered him in the local county fair diaper derby. My younger brother had gone with me. The race took place on a stage that had footlights. My brother held Allen at the start line and I was at the finished line. When the race began, Allen was heading toward me, as I was joyfully calling to him. Not one baby noticed the lights, except Allen. I was hoping to get his attention by yelling his name. Instead, Allen headed for the lights. My brother had to run after him and pick him up, before he fell off the stage.

In the summer of 1986, I had joined Ron in Illinois. Allen was a year old then, and he was not walking. He showed signs of being able to walk. He was a very strong baby and could climb out of his crib and playpen. Occasionally, Allen would fall hitting his head. He always seemed fine after these accidents. When Allen was seventeen months old, I took him to a pediatrician on the naval base. She gave him several different tests to check his mental ability. Allen was borderline on most of the tests, except one. The doctor was not able to offer an explanation for the high score. She felt that he was slow, but could walk. If Allen did not walk by the time he was eighteen months old, he would have to go through physical therapy. Even though, the doctor had evidence to support borderline intelligence in my son, I felt that these tests were not reliable. Two weeks later, Allen was walking.

Allen did have some peculiarities, which was nothing to do with his intelligence. He was very sensitive to sound and distracted by visual stimuli. Getting Allen away from something that had his visual attention, was difficult. Allen enjoyed putting puzzles together and creating gadgets with his legos.

In December of 1986, Ron finished 'A' School in Electronics and was sent to another location to continue his program of study. We went home to visit my parents. On Christmas Eve, we were traveling to visit my younger brother and his wife. At an intersection, a car driven by an elderly woman, ran into the passenger side of our car where Allen was sitting in his car seat. It was a hard impact that sent us into a tail spin. Ron had hurt his leg and still has recurring problems with it. Lisa had hit her head on the metal part of Allen's safety seat and has to this day a bone bruise on her forehead. I was shaken up some and Allen miraculously seemed fine. He was not crying and appeared dazed, but he was conscious. We went to the nearest hospital and had the children examined. Allen could have slung forward in his car seat and then slung back hard hitting the back of his head. I thought he was fine. Later, Allen would begin to show dramatic changes in his speech and motor skills.

When Allen was three, he had a great vocabulary. He spoke in complete sentences and was a helper around the house. Whenever Ron was fixing things, Allen would go and get the tools needed. Allen showed courtesy by opening doors for others and helped put groceries away. For two years, he took over as the older child.

They knew Allen at his preschool of being the brightest child. As mentioned previously, Allen began his preschool years two weeks before his second birthday. On his first day, he unlocked the back door in his classroom and let all of the children outside to play. They told me that no other child had ever figured out the lock on the door. The preschool liked him, since he never gave them any trouble, except the incident with the door.

Allen did have a problem with his shoelaces. He was always losing them. I had to purchase a bag of shoelaces, just so he would have a new pair to use every day. When I questioned the staff about it, they thought that he was burying them outside in the sand.

When Allen was three years old, his class put on a Christmas program. Allen was the only child, who had memorized all of the songs for the program. He was not intimidated and sung in front of everyone. He had 'personality' and was able to talk to anyone. He loved hugs and kisses. Then, the only problem Allen had, was with his potty training. Allen was attached to his diaper. It was a comfort zone for him. Allen had the same problem with his bottle. Eventually, he realized that he liked the taste of Sprite, which would only be served in a cup. Therefore, he gave up his bottle. As for his potty-training, I bought Allen special underwear. His favorite was the kind with the Disney characters printed on them. Also, he liked to play with zippers. If Allen had on his special underwear and wore a pair of pants with a zipper, he had no trouble using the toilet. Unfortunately, at night, Allen returned to his diaper. Someone had told us not to give him any fluids before bedtime and that would stop the problem. This method worked off and on.

When Allen was four years old, Ron was involved in the Persian Gulf War. He was sent overseas on a battleship. I thought at first when Allen began to act differently, that he was showing signs of regressing. Lisa had drooled and began wetting her pants, when Allen was first born. Allen showed the same signs of doing this, except that he carried his left arm and dragged his feet. Allen would also stutter and not look at anyone when he was speaking. His eyes would roll upwards. I guessed I truly did not know what caused this. I was working a full-time job and had two other children to contend with. I was constantly worried about Ron. At times, I had problems doing the simplest things, like paying bills on time, etc. Maybe, subconsciously, I just did not want to deal with Allen's unusual problems. The crime I committed was not taking him to a doctor and having him examined. When Ron came back from the Persian Gulf War, I had expected a change in Allen, which I did not see.

When Allen entered kindergarten, he attended the same school at which I taught at, just like Lisa. Allen was given speech therapy and retained for being developmentally-delayed. He was not able to skip, jump or hop. When he went outside to play, he was more interested in the butterflies and caterpillars.

During his second time in kindergarten, I began to work with him. Ron would watch Lisa and Kim. Allen did not have any problem with reading, but he did with fine and gross motor skills. I took him to the park as much as possible, hoping to stimulate him in physical activities.

I felt that Allen would eventually catch up, but that he would never be an athlete. The worst had not happened to Allen, yet. It was just beginning.

Chapter Five

Diagnosis of Moderate Cerebral Palsy

The worst year of my life began when Allen entered first grade. Allen did show an increase in his ability to communicate orally, although sometimes he still drifted. He still qualified for speech therapy and was receiving those services. He had problems with penmanship. At the beginning of the year, he was not able to write across his paper. It would always drift down. Later, this did improve. He had constant problems with gross motor skills, especially during P.E. Later, I learned that he was always being ridiculed and forced to do physical activities that he was not able to do. Finally, came the day I would never forget! It was in April of 1994. It was toward the end of my teaching day, that the parent technician came to my room and told me that the principal needed to see me. I went very confused, since they had never summoned me like that before. When I entered her office, our two guidance counselors were there. I was informed that Allen had a nervous breakdown on the gym floor. He had talked about wanting to kill himself. His classroom teacher had helped him to get up and leave the gym. She took him directly to the guidance counselor's office. That particular guidance counselor had several pages of written notes concerning the conversation she had with Allen. Allen had described the way he wanted to kill himself and that he heard voices. She labeled him psychotic. Legally, she should not have voiced her view. She is only able to describe the incident and nothing more. A medical doctor is allowed to diagnose and label a child. Ultimately, she was determined to bring Allen up to our child study team and have him placed in special education for the emotionally disturbed. The principal suggested that I take him to an outside source and have him evaluated. The other guidance counselor remained quiet the entire time, which I thought was unusual. After that year, she left the school system. Later, the guidance counselor, who labeled Allen, became an assistant principal at another school. Later, she left the school system.

After this meeting, I took Allen straight home. We had a private conversation away from his other siblings. I asked him what had happened. Allen had explained that the children were laughing at him when he tried to skip. He had fallen and began to cry. He used the expression about killing himself. I asked him if he really wanted to do that and he had said 'no'. He looked at me as if I were crazy for asking him that. Furthermore, the guidance counselor had asked him how he was going to kill himself and he described a scene from a movie that he had seen. He knew that if he continued talking about it, then he would not have to go back to class and face the other students. The idea of him hearing voices was really not true. Allen had very sensitive hearing. We have neighbors, who sometimes talk to each other in their yards and Allen can hear their conversations. To this day, Allen cannot handle listening to most music. He has to plug-up his ears, with his hands, to block out the noise.

Unfortunately, the seed had been planted at school about Allen. I immediately set up an appointment through Champus. I wanted to keep the child study team at bay, if possible. The consultant recommended a psychiatrist for Allen. I went to him several times and eventually he tested Allen. From the results of the test, Allen was mildly retarded in certain areas and had ADHD. Most of the tests consisted of verbal responses and because Allen was inattentive, he must have ADHD. Allen did show signs of being active on trips. Any new place that he went to, he was hard to handle. He had to touch and feel just about everything that he saw. The most popular thing for him was playing with the elevator. He had to push all of the buttons and spend time going up and down the elevator. Sometimes, when he had to urinate, he did not use the restroom. Once with his class on a field trip, he stood behind a tree and did it. Another time he was with me in the supermarket and he was standing behind me and did it. I had heard the sound of it and turned around to witness the incident. When I brought him home, I had him sit in a chair and think about what he had done. He never did it again, as far as I knew.

Sometimes, Allen would take off running for no apparent reason and I would have to take off after him. Although, he did show some signs of having ADHD, it did not explain several issues. When he was used to going to a particular place, he was calm. He could keep his attention for long periods on certain tasks. From my professional experience with ADHD, the child is always active. For several years, I played with the label, because it was better than psychotic.

The child study team met and decided that Allen was developmentally delayed and had ADHD. They suggested that I continue to take Allen to see the psychiatrist. The counselor was still adamant about Allen's placement. She had taken out her notes and had shared her findings with the team. She mentioned Allen hearing voices and about our cat going through a hole in the wall. On that last remark, I could explain. Our cat, Duchess, did go through an opening in the wall. It was where we kept our items for storage. The counselor did have a convincing case. Luckily, Allen's teacher did not go along with the term of 'psychotic'. She stated that he was not a problem in the classroom and that he was an honor roll student. The team decided that Allen did not qualify for special education.

I was relieved to hear their decision, but not satisfied. I finally accepted the fact that there was something terribly wrong with Allen. He needed some kind of physical therapy, since his main problems came from not being able to do gross motor activities. I was not as worried about his communication skills, since obvious signs showed he was improving. As I continued my quest to find the answers, the little boy I had remembered in preschool, no longer existed. I had no evidence to prove how he was when he was little. Perhaps, I should have kept a daily journal, because that would have been my only link to the past.

To help improve Allen's agility, I enrolled Allen in a local beginning swimming course. The idea of enrolling him in swimming came from watching the 1992 Olympics. A swimmer, from Australia, had suffered a leg injury as a young child. He began taking swimming lessons to improve the strength in his leg. Allen began his lessons in the spring, during first grade. He attended ten weekly lessons held on Saturday. His instructor was a young woman and she could not get Allen into the pool. I did not want to push Allen, so I allowed him to sit on the side of the pool and watch the other kids. After five lessons, Allen was still not in the water. On lesson number six, his dad attended. He yelled at Allen to get into the water. Allen was more afraid of his dad than the water, so he got in. It was quite embarrassing, but it worked. Allen had difficulty using his left arm and leg. It was so obvious, when the instructor was working with him. Also, Allen had a problem with getting his face wet. He refused to duck under the water. Even though, the other children made progress and some advanced to the next level, I was comfortable with leaving Allen in his current swimming status. He would stay with the program, until he learned to swim.

One day as I was waiting outside the boys' locker room for Allen, I over heard a conversation. Some boys had ganged up on Allen, because he was talking strangely. They threatened to hit him with their metal baskets and probably would have, if I had not been standing behind them witnessing the entire scene. From that moment on, I was protective of Allen. He no longer changed in the boys' locker room. Instead, he wore his swim trunks to the pool. He would dry off and leave the pool, wearing his wet trunks. I did complain to the pool's manager about the incident and later they replaced the metal baskets with lockers.

Allen had a total of six sessions with his psychiatrist and with all of this testing, it accumulated to more than ten thousand dollars. I was relieved that the program under Champus, known as 'Preferred Choice,' covered these expenses. Still, in my heart, I was not close to discovering Allen's problem. I was concerned about Allen's left side. I did not understand why he was weak on that side. He could barely hop on his left foot. If he went around objects on his left side, he would fall down. His psychiatrist was his provider under this program and I had to insist that Allen have an examination. The psychiatrist recommended a pediatrician that was in the same building.

I went to Dr. L. and while we were waiting, Allen did the most unusual thing. It began with Allen and me sharing a book together. Right after reading the book, Allen could give me a complete summary of the story using adult vocabulary, while comparing it with another story he had read in the past. I never truly realized how bright he was, until I saw the amazed look on the other parents' faces. Since I was a teacher with more than ten years' experience, I should have known that Allen was showing remarkable speaking and high reasoning skills. Yet, Allen had done this before occasionally. I was so absorbed in looking at his weaknesses that I did not venture into his strengths. Allen did not use adult vocabulary, when he was confronted with material that had no visual stimuli, such as books without pictures or oral conversations. Instead, he drifted back to simple sentences and drifted off the subject.

When we saw the doctor, I thought for sure he would see how clumsy Allen was. He had Allen hop on his left foot. Allen was only able to do it twice and then fall down. On his right leg, he hopped six times. When Allen was asked to sit on the bed, he tried to get on it from his left side. He was not able to, so he had to do it on his right side. It was mentioned to the doctor about Allen's verbal ability with visual clues and then without it. Dr. L thought that Allen was developmentally-delayed and that he would catch up. At that point, I saw 'RED'. Controlling my temper was very difficult.

When I met with the psychiatrist, I told him that I was not happy with Dr. L's results. I demanded that I see a different doctor. While the psychiatrist recommended another pediatrician, a voice from within me cried out, 'neurologist.' I asked to take Allen to see a neurologist and the psychiatrist had agreed.

During this time, Allen had begun his second session for swimming lessons. I bought him a pair of goggles, so he would not get his eyes wet. He did not like to wear the goggles at first. He simply enjoyed splashing around in the water like an infant and he seldom paid attention to the male instructor. One day it was raining outside and a small leak was in the sunroof. Hearing the drops falling in the water was difficult. None of the other children paid any attention to it, except Allen. He slowly wandered over to where it was hitting the water. The male instructor was so upset with Allen's lack of attention that he splashed water on Allen. Some of it went into Aaron's eyes. His face turned beet red and I thought he was going to cry. Instead, he swam the length of the pool to get away from the instructor. He swam perfectly! Anyone who saw him would think nothing was wrong with him. Yet, later he regressed back to the way he was, except he began to participate more. He learned to skip. When that incident occurred, Ron took the training wheels off Allen's bike. Ron did not have that much patience with Allen's inattentiveness. Allen would spend a great deal of his time watching ants and butterflies, instead of trying to ride his bike. Finally, Ron got mad at Allen and made him learn to ride the bike. Within three days, Allen was riding his bike. He rode it very slowly watching for insects on the road. I have never seen anyone ride a bike so slowly! One day, near our house, Allen watched a caterpillar crawling for more than two hours. Sometimes, his attention span amazed me.

It took six long weeks, before we could see a neurologist. Dr. F. was a turning point for Allen's medical diagnosis. Dr. F. observed Allen and thought that he was developmentally-delayed and needed to be in an adaptive P.E. class. He recommended swimming and learning to play the piano. Piano lessons would strengthen Allen's finger dexterity. He diagnosed Allen with mild autism and ADD. I continued with Allen's swimming lessons and during Allen's third session he learned to float. He absolutely loved floating! He learned to use his goggles and was thrilled at holding his breath underwater. I began to see signs of Allen using his left leg more, and his arm.

Having Allen practice for his piano lessons was difficult. We used the piano in the school's auditorium, and he would only practice ten minutes a day. He took lessons at the local recreational center. He had other students in the class with him and he had trouble concentrating. The sound of the other students practicing, disturbed him greatly. Naturally, the instructor recommended private lessons. Instead, I asked the instructor to have Allen perform first and dismiss him. He did this for quite sometime and it helped. Allen did make progress in his lessons.

In second grade, Allen was on the B-average honor roll, twice. He was making good academic progress, but daydreamed and had difficulty putting his thoughts on paper. He shined in mathematics and was at the top of his class. His teacher noticed that he had a great memory and could confer information that he had read about, if it were of nonfictional content. Frequently, he shook his left arm, whenever, he was excited about something. Sometimes, he would cross his eyes and shake his head, before entering a crowded area, such as the auditorium or cafeteria. I reported these incidences to Dr. F. He had Allen take an EEG at a children's hospital and had a hearing evaluation done, too. The EEG showed no problems, but his hearing evaluation proved that he had unusual sharp hearing. Dr. F. advised that Allen wear ear plugs to drown out the loud noise. Unfortunately, I could not get Allen to wear them.

Allen continued to take swimming lessons for five years. He slowly made more improvements and eventually he made it to the top group. He swam very slowly and was not able to compete in races. Although, both of his sisters became competitive in this area. Allen remained a faithful participant at the open recreational swimming, when it became available.

It was in third grade, when he began to be disruptive in class. This behavior was prompted by his inability to participate in writing assignments. He was referred again, to the child study team. Since he was high in math and low in writing skills, I thought he might have a chance to receive services for learning disabled. I decided not to use the school's evaluation team, but went with a referral from Dr.F. to have Allen tested. The entire evaluation took one whole day and Allen was seen by a neuropsychologist and his team. The test's results showed weaknesses in certain areas and Allen was a prime candidate as having a learning disability. Allen was also wetting the bed and he was taking medication for this problem. Allen's medical diagnoses remained with the labeling of mild autism and ADD.

The school psychologist and diagnostician were adamant in trying to place Allen in the emotionally-disturbed class under special education. Since they listed Allen with mild autism, they immediately wanted him where the other autistic children were placed. An actual placement for children with autism in this school system did not exist. They were all placed in the emotionally-disturbed classes. Although, they told me that they had different kinds of classes arranged under this category. I was not comfortable with this issue. These two individuals were not familiar with the term of autism. In fact, many different categories of this disorder existed and they were not aware of it. I guess that making a round peg fit in a square hole was easier for them. I guess it is possible, when ignorance is the hammer.

I had met the psychologist before, at a meeting for parents that had autistic children. She was the parent with two autistic children, both of them younger than Allen. Naturally, she thought he should be placed with this label, because her children were. Later, she was very wrong in making quick assumptions.

The label of emotionally-disturbed would always be on his record and he would always be judged by that label and not by his disability. A no-way situation existed.

I refused to sign the papers that the diagnostician gave me and I told her off. I asked her if she really knew and understood the different categories of autism. She admitted that she did not. The psychologist remained silent. Not throwing the papers at them was difficult. Surprisingly, the diagnostician and I became friends later.

The third grade teacher had convincing evidence that Allen needed to receive some form of counseling. He was still inattentive during writing sessions and caused disruptive problems at P.E. They did not offer him the adaptive P.E. that his doctor requested. When I brought up the issue, the paperwork requesting adaptive P.E., was missing from his cumulative record. I learned a hard lesson. From now on, I would always make sure that anything I received from a doctor, I would make a copy of. I began to keep all documentation on file.

I went to the principal over the issue and she asked the P.E. teacher to allow Allen to sit out, whenever he felt uncomfortable about doing a task. One would have thought that this P.E. teacher would have done that. She had known Allen's history with gross motor skills.

From Allen's inattentiveness, Dr. F. put Allen on dexedrine. He did not recommend retalin, although, that was the commonly described medication. Allen received dexedrine because he had a sleep disorder, along with his bed-wetting. Allen began to lose weight and constantly complained about the back of his legs hurting him. He had trouble sitting on the piano bench, during practice. I had to obtain a more comfortable chair for him to sit in, during the school day. Sometimes, he would have to lie on the floor in the classroom. Frequently, he became very grouchy and no one wanted to be around him. The principal assumed I was taking him to see a private therapist for his behavior. I truly thought that it would not do any good. Something inside me, would not let me.

One day Allen had a blotchy red rash under his arms. On that day he was wearing shorts and he had the same painful rash on the back of his legs. I immediately took him to a nearby medical clinic and learned that something was disturbing his white blood cell count. They told me to take him off the dexedrine, immediately! Allen should have been weaned off this medicine. Unfortunately, Allen gained a huge amount of weight. He acquired more than fifty pounds. He had a difficult time controlling his new eating habit and would sneak into the refrigerator at night. It did not matter to him what he ate. He just wanted to eat.

When he saw Dr. F. again, I was told to put Allen on a diet. I was very careful in selecting the food we ate. Nevertheless, it did not matter. Allen ate too much of everything. Now, participating in P.E. was even more difficult. During his fourth-grade year, the same P.E. teacher was hard on him. She wanted him to lose weight and made sure that he participated as much as possible. Besides dealing with his weight, Allen had to handle criticism from his peers. He became more of a loner. Ron would take him for walks in the evening, but it did not help. Allen simply did not have the desire to lose the weight. He had given up.

It was his babysitter that came to his aid. She watched my children in the morning, so that they could walk to school and become part of the neighborhood. She had known Allen, since he was two years old. He had been going to her house in the mornings daily, when he began kindergarten. Mrs. Lee loved him. He would talk vigorously around her and she would listen to him. So, when Allen improved in speaking more effectively, she received the credit.

When Allen began fifth-grade, Mrs. Lee's grandson was in the same class. He had a reputation of being tough and the other children left Allen alone. Allen weighed 180 pounds and it looked like it was not going to come off. Since I had learned about the 504 Plan from dealing with Lisa, I was adamant about pursuing one for Allen. I was determined to get him on one, before he began middle school. He could not handle regular P.E. The thought kept me up at nights.

I went back to see Dr. F. and told him my concerns. Dr. F. began to believe that Allen did not have mild autism, since he could swim and showed an increase in his speaking skills. Children, with any form of autism, would not have made the progress that Allen had made. I felt that Allen showed more signs of a traumatic head injury.

Allen received further testing from the same neuropsychologist and his team. This time they did more testing and discovered that Allen had mild cerebral palsy. The neuropsychologist felt that it came from an injury to the base of Allen's skull, that could have happened from a fall or car accident. Dr. F. felt that it was prenatal.

At the end of the fifth-grade, Allen had his 504 Plan in place. They would give him specific classroom accommodations and adaptive P.E. I began to see that Allen showed signs of possibly having cerebral palsy. His hands would wave, whenever, he was excited about something. He walked with a gait and could not do cursive writing, since his wrists were not flexible. I observed him trying to run one day and saw that he had little flexibility in his ankles. Dr. F. had explained to me that no one knows enough about the human brain and in Allen's case, who knows what he could do as the years progress. I felt that Allen's problem was a traumatic brain injury and that the brain compensates for what the injured part cannot do. That would explain the unusual way that Allen would learn to do something, like riding his bike and skipping. Allen began to write effectively on any given subject, but he still was not able to do cursive writing.

Later, I realized that Allen's brain injury may have not come from that car accident in his earlier years. In fact, the injury may have occurred later. I remembered one day going into the preschool that Allen had attended and picking up Kim. Kim was four years old at the time and her teacher had a child in the air shaking her vigorously. I immediately reported it to the director. The teacher was old enough to retire and so she did. Kim had admitted that she never shook her. But, what about Allen? She had been his teacher when he was two years old. Sure enough, she had shaken him. He never told me, because he did not want to get her into trouble.

The continual problems at P.E. had been ongoing. He nearly received a conduct notice for not participating in double-dutch jumping. I had placed in Allen's cum record another copy of a letter from Dr. F., requesting that Allen receive adaptive P.E. services. Again, it was missing. The principal stepped in again, and spoke with the P.E. teacher. All of this occurred, before Allen was labeled with cerebral palsy.

The P.E. teacher was not the only misunderstanding soul. A newly hired guidance counselor was worse. Only one explanation could explain the event that I am about to describe. The principal asked her to do it. Since Aaron was labeled with cerebral palsy, I requested that he be offered a 504 Plan. The principal wanted him in a special educational program, so that she would never be held liable. She knew about 504 Plans and never offered this information to me. Allen should have qualified for one, when he was first labeled with a disability, such as ADHD. If Allen were in a special educational program, then there would be less likelihood of a lawsuit. When a child is on the 504 Plan, it comes with the hidden meaning of compensatory damages, if they do not follow it. What had occurred one day behind closed doors, in the guidance counselor's office, was inexcusable. She attempted to provoke Allen into having a nervous breakdown. She yelled at him. She told him repeatedly that there was something wrong with him, since he did not want to make friends with the other kids. Allen did have few friends, with the help of Mrs. Lee's grandson. I would never have learned about this occurrence, if it had not been for the guidance counselor telling me. Several days after the incident, she came to me, telling me that Allen needed more help than what she could provide. I asked her why she felt compelled to offer my son counseling, when I did not request it. I learned later that it did not come from his classroom teacher, either. Naturally, I asked Allen about it. He told me that she was trying to get him upset and something told him to hang in there, which was a wise move on his part. Their desire to label him 'emotionally disturbed' was apparent. Once when he received the diagnosis of 'cerebral palsy', everyone should have stepped in and offer the required assistance of a 504 Plan.

It turned out that the guidance counselor was known for having emotional outbursts. She would cry at a drop of a hat. In fact, she was seeing a therapist for her own problems. Imagine, someone like that, was working in the position of a guidance counselor. Later, she moved away to join her husband, who had received a job transfer.

Allen was placed on a 504 Plan at the end of that school year. He looked forward to middle school and we thought he would be given new opportunities. I naively thought that a 504 Plan would take care of his problems. Well, it did not. He and I had some more growing up to do!

Chapter Six

Juvenile Glaucoma Goes Undiagnosed
(Kim's Birth and Preschool Years)

Kim was my third child born by Caesarian birth. I knew exactly when Kim had been conceived. It was another unplanned pregnancy. I was using the rhythm method and the pages on my personal calendar had stuck together. Therefore, I had missed up on the count. According to my calculations, the birth of Kim should be in August. I had an ultrasound test to decide the approximate arrival date. The results showed that Kim should be born in September. Later, I had another one done and it still showed the same results. My doctor was very comfortable in waiting until September, while I was not. This would be my third Caesarian and not going into labor was important for me. A Caesarian birth should take place two weeks before the expectancy date. Therefore, knowing the approximate date was very important. My doctor arranged for me to have an amniocentesis to decide the infant's status. They told me that if I did not have it done, he would not schedule an arrival date for Kim. I would just have to go into labor. Then, I had no choice. The test was done on August 19th. They inserted a long needle into my abdomen and it was witnessed by a new doctor, an experienced one and by an intern. The needle accidentally stuck into Kim, which I did not see. The intern was the one, who mentioned that they had poked the infant with the needle, when she moved. It supposedly poked her in the ankle. They realized by the fluid of the womb, that Kim was ready to be born. They felt that she would weigh around six pounds. Two days later, I was admitted to the hospital and a seven pound, six ounce baby girl was born. Naturally, the first thing I did when I held her, was to see where she had been poked. The only mark I saw on her, was on her face. It was a reddish mark between her nose and her mouth. When I was recovering in the hospital, a team of four people dressed in white hospital garments examined me. They were mostly concerned about my legs. Immediately, after they left, my physician came in and examined me. I told him that they had just examined me. Apparently, it was not from his staff, nor the hospital's. So, who were they? Later, I had to fill out a lengthy questionnaire about my amniocentesis for my insurance company. They were questioning the reason this test was given and so late in my pregnancy. Within that year, my physician had retired.

The only ailment that Kim developed was jaundice. She was a lovely baby that followed the normal progression of development. She did not have colic and slept the average number of hours that an infant sleeps. Kim was the perfect baby. I had learned early that Kim was an avid visual learner. When Kim was four weeks old, I had to return to work or jeopardize my teaching contract. I was lucky to find a child care provider that only had another infant to take care of. From my experience, I instinctly felt comfortable with this provider. She took care of Kim, until Kim was ready for preschool.

Kim was the typical child that one could raise by reading child care books, except for one thing. Kim was a born entertainer. At her preschool, she would get on top of the tabletops and sing to the other kids. She was exceptional in her oral ability and had a keen insight in dealing with others.

During her preschool years, she was a dream. She experienced only the regular problems that a preschooler would have. I never suspected that she had a disability and would eventually have far more problems to deal with, than her older brother and sister.

Chapter Seven

Juvenile Glaucoma, Dyslexia and Scotopic Sensitivity Awareness

In kindergarten, she made average progress, except not knowing a few letters of the alphabet. She was passed on to first grade and later received additional help in reading. I may have been blind to Kim's academic needs, since that was the same year that Allen had his emotional breakdown. Kim was having problems in reading and writing. Sometimes, she would write everything backwards. They decided that Kim was not mature enough to go onto second grade. She did make successful strides in repeating first grade.

During her second year in first grade, Kim would complained about not being able to see the board. She had said the same thing the previous year. Again, I had the nurse give Kim a visual eye screening. The process was done by using a Snellen Eye Chart. Both times, Kim had 20/20 sight and should not be experiencing any problems. At least, that is what I thought. However, since Kim occasionally wrote backwards, I decided to take her to an ophthalmologist. He tested Kim's vision and found her to have only a slight vision problem, not enough for glasses. As for her problem with writing, he felt that it was only a maturity problem and that she would outgrow it. He would see her again in two years.

I had made two mistakes in dealing with Kim's undiagnosed problem. First, I should never have relied on the Snellen Chart results given by the school nurse. She was not trained in dealing with visual problems. The use of the Snellen Eye Chart's sole purpose is to decide whether one is nearly blind or not. The other mistake I made, was not really listening to Kim. I made quick decisions when it came to her welfare, and unjustly labeled her as a slow learner. I knew that she showed signs of having dyslexia and took after her father. Ron always had difficulty with reading.

During her second grade year, Kim did not make the strides for which I had hoped. She made some gains in reading, but her writing was atrocious. In the second grade, children learn to adjust to using notebook paper. Kim could not use notebook paper. Her writing was very large and clumsy. Ultimately, when she entered third grade she was suffering. She was tested and placed back in a second grade reader and received additional help by participating in an after-school reading program.

Since Kim was at risk of repeating third grade, I took her to see an optometrist, who specialized in visual disorders. He had Kim do a series of tests and I was surprised to learn that Kim showed signs of having high intellectual intelligence. Her problem was dyslexia and she would need to go through a visual therapy program. Our insurance did not cover the costs and so we had to pay for the entire expense. Since I was a teacher, the optometrist had me receive some training from a vision specialist, so I could work with Kim at home. Kim was recommended for bifocals to aid in her reading, which I invested in. Kim received six months of vision therapy, before I decided not to continue these services.

Kim continued to complain about not being able to see what she was writing on her paper. She wrote with a leaded pencil on notebook paper. She would become so frustrated, that she would crumple the paper and start again. One day there was a huge pile on the floor and a teary-eyed Kim. She simply had trouble writing. The vision specialist could not tell me what was wrong with Kim, and neither could the optometrist. Around that same time, I received a card in the mail for Kim's vision checkup by the ophthalmologist. I decided to take Kim, along with samples of her work.

I took Kim to a late appointment, one that followed her lengthy school day, which included her attendance at the after-school reading program. The ophthalmologist was concerned about her school work, but more about her eye pressure. Apparently, he was so concerned that he had the back of Kim's eyes photographed. The first time it was done, there was not a clear picture. The process to get a clear picture was very time-consuming. Eventually, Kim had to return five different times, before the ophthalmologist was satisfied. They told me that everything was fine and that he would see Kim for a checkup.

Two weeks later, I received a phone call at school. It surprised me to hear from the ophthalmologist. He had told me that he had carefully analyzed the results and Kim had glaucoma. Since he primarily worked with older adults with glaucoma, he referred me to another doctor that handled children with juvenile glaucoma. We saw this doctor, who came highly-recommended, several times. His diagnosis of Kim was entirely different. Her eye pressure reading was normal to borderline. He felt that she did not have glaucoma. Yet, since it fluctuated, he recommended medication to relieve eye stress. I mentioned Kim's difficulty with seeing her writing on paper. He recommended that I see a learning disability consultant and that was that.

I went back to the first ophthalmologist and stated what had occurred. From that moment on, he became Kim's eye care professional. He examined Kim and her pressure readings were high and recommended medication to ease the pressure. High eye pressure can cause damage to the optic nerve and it is permanent.

Kim went to fifth-grade on a 504 Plan. Dr. H. had written a letter giving her a diagnosis of juvenile glaucoma. He included some suggestions for classroom accommodations provided in a book about juvenile glaucoma. The Glaucoma Research Foundation published the book. Although, she was on a 504 Plan, she was still having problems in reading and writing. She was again placed back a year in her reading level. I still began to question the reasons why. Kim was not a great oral reader, but she could comprehend very well. Finally, I began to realize that maybe it had nothing to do with Kim's ability, but more in what she saw on paper. The more advanced a student became in reading, the smaller the print would be. So, if Kim had a vision problem, she would have trouble reading smaller print.

Finally, came the time when I experienced a shocking revelation about Kim. This event occurred in my classroom, one day after school. Kim was having problems doing long division. So, I wrote a division problem on the board. Kim showed a weakness in lining up the numbers to solve the problem. I had her solve the problem on the board and go to her desk and copy it on her paper. As she sat there, I noticed that she was not writing. So, I asked her why she did not copy down the problem. Kim remarked that something was blocking her vision. I questioned her about how that was possible, since nothing was in her line of sight. Kim described that all she could see was white. She had to wait for it to disappear, before she could copy from the board.

I began to notice that at home Kim always sat in front of the television. When I asked her why, she told me that the picture would be distorted when she sat away from it. Kim began to complain about headaches and dots that she would see. I wanted answers to these real concerns.

I took Kim back again to Dr. H. (her ophthalmologist). She was given a wide-range test and a contrast-sensitivity test. She passed the first test, but the other she did not completely pass. She saw horizontal gray lines, but not the vertical lines shown in the pictures. Yet, when I mentioned this to Dr. H., he did not give any comment. He had stated that he thought she was psychosomatic and did not have a physical problem. I saw 'red' and finally Dr. H. admitted to me that he did not know what it was. Then, the only thing that he could help me with was her eye pressure.

I decided on my own to see Dr. F. (Allen's neurologist). I thought that maybe it was a problem with her optic nerve. Dr. F. asked Kim lots of questions and took a serious look at Kim. He was not sure what it was, but wanted her to have an EEG done and to see Dr. B for psychological testing. Once when these tests were taken, Kim would go back to see him. During that time, I scheduled a restudy of Kim with the child study team at my school. I did not look forward to speaking with them concerning Kim. Previously, I had met with them three times, before Kim was given a 504 Plan. They had wanted classroom strategies from her medical doctor and not just a diagnosis. Actually, that was their way of hoping that I could not get these accommodations written in a medical letter and therefore, not be able to obtain a 504 Plan. It was a game they were playing. They had played this game with others. One day I heard two members of the team discussing a child with severe asthma. They were laughing about the situation, because they knew that the parent probably could not obtain a suggestion for classroom accommodations in the child's letter of diagnosis. They remarked that it was not a medical doctor's position to include these suggestions in a letter of diagnosis. Since they would only accept a medical doctor's opinion, the parent would have difficulty in her quest. If this were an example of what a child study team was capable of doing, then there was no telling how many parents would get frustrated in their attempts to obtain a 504 Plan for their child.

I had learned from Dr. F. that there was a possibility that Kim could have dyslexia. How the brain receives visual stimuli causes dyslexia. I have seen some of my students with symptoms of dyslexia. Many different types of dyslexia exist. It is a shame that my school system did not test for it. With all the big fuss about increasing students' academic knowledge and pouring more into the curriculum, like a sponge soaking up water, there should have been the consideration for those students that have a hidden disability. The problem lies with our society refusing to deal with students that have a learning problem. So, when they increase the workload to challenge students, it will become even more difficult for a student that has a learning problem. Kim's current future did not look bright.

Dr. F. wanted to know why I brought Kim to see him. He was stunned to learn that the school system did not test for dyslexia. Students, who qualify, are placed in a LD program or labeled a slow learner. A slow learner would repeat grades or be placed. In the LD program, the pace of the required work is slowed, but no special teaching methods are used. In my experience, I had seen different methods of instruction being used with LD students and it was effective. Since I was familiar with the LD program for my school system, I did not want Kim placed in it.

Some students that I knew that were in the LD program never graduated from high school. They were placed in a training program and only received a certificate of attendance. The thought of going to college was nonexistent. They did not offer them many choices.

Kim's future seemed very bleak. Although, she was on a 504 Plan, her accommodations were not enough. Kim's problem seemed complicated and would take a great deal of time in diagnosing it. One day I was surfing the Internet and came across an article about scotopic sensitivity. Some people have trouble filtering light through their optic nerve. This applies to flourescent light that buildings use. There was a simple test with fourteen symptoms. Kim had twelve of those symptoms. Now, I was on the verge of learning more about Kim's problem, but with no one in our state that was trained. I downloaded the information that I could find and took it with me, when Kim went for her psychological evaluation from Dr. B.

Before Kim went for her appointment with Dr. B., Lisa had lost her glasses and had to have them replaced. While we were at the optician's office, we saw a display of colored lenses. On the Internet, the doctor who discovered this disorder, had mentioned using colored lens. A pair of colored lenses helped to filter out the glare from light and made it easier for a person to read. Each individual was tested to see which color suited them best. I told the optician about scotopic sensitivity and he seemed receptive to what I said. He sold a product that completely blocked out glare. It was a coating placed on the lens. He showed me a sample lens with the coating and I was shocked at the difference it made, when I looked through it. He mentioned about colors and how important a pair of colored lenses along with the special glare coating, could be helpful. Although, he had not heard of this disorder, he did say that twenty years ago when flourescent lighting was first invented, some inventors wore pink lenses because of the glare. He heard only about it a short time and then nothing was ever said again about the use of pink lenses.

It was strange that Kim was always attached to the color pink. I remembered once that she had a pair of sunglasses that had pink lenses. She loved wearing them. I had thought at the time that Kim was obsessed with pink. Little did I know, that Kim was trying to adapt to her problem.

We went back to Dr. H and had an updated checkup. Dr. H. agreed that Kim needed a new pair of lenses. I did not tell him about the special glasses I had in mind. All I cared about, was obtaining the prescription from him and how her eye pressure was doing. At the time, Kim's medication was up to date and her pressure reading was good.

Finally, the time came for Kim to see Dr.B. Kim experienced an entire day of being given various tests, by trained professionals. Dr. B. had conferenced with Kim and then with me. He had asked about Allen and was interested in learning more about Lisa. Since Allen and Lisa were presently doing fine in school, he questioned whether their so-called problems were family-oriented rather than medical. He had asked about any drastic changes in our family life. For example, more income or a better neighborhood to live in. It was highly unusual for Allen and Lisa to be showing stronger academic performance as they had become older. Generally, students with disabilities struggle in their academic endeavors, when they get older. I do not think he realized what an important asset the 504 Plan has in making or breaking a student's success. Furthermore,. he wondered why Kim was not a behavioral problem in school, if she were having difficulties. Over the years, I had worked toward building my children's self-esteem. For Kim, her strongest assets were singing, playing certain sports and using her hands. For her singing, I had her enter the PTA Reflections Contest. In kindergarten, Kim received second-place at her school. In first grade, she received first place at her school, first place in the city and third place in the district. In second grade, she received first place at her school and then won second place in the city. In third grade, the school did not compete. In fourth-grade, Kim received first-place at her school, first-place in the city and third-place in the district. In fifth-grade, Kim again received first place at her school and first-place in the city. These competitions were terrific for building Kim's self-esteem.

Kim had been taking swimming lessons, since she was four. They had nicknamed her the 'minnow.' She became involved with the local swim team and had various ribbons for first, second and third place. She had been very proud of her accomplishments in learning new techniques in the backstroke, front crawl and her favorite the butterfly. When Kim was younger, she was involved in ballet, karate and bowling.

Another gift Kim has is her 'sunshine' personality. She is a very pretty girl and had two different artists request to paint her face on canvas. Kim had entered the pageant scene, but the cost of dresses and entry fees were too expensive. Instead, Kim became involved in community service. She joined an organization known as 'Young Girls in Focus.' Kim became involved with helping the homeless, visiting senior citizens' retirement homes and learning how to take care of infants.

Kim's other talent was with her hands. Even as a young child, she always had to touch things. She began to show a talent for drawing and doing pottery. Her father wanted her to become involved in cooking, since she had a knack in precise cutting.

As I waited to learn the results of Kim's psychological and intelligence tests, I spoke with her fifth-grade teacher. Kim needed to take breaks in the afternoon and I was concerned about the glare in the classroom. Her teacher was very concerned about Kim passing the state-required tests that would have an impact on her promotion. I told her that once when I receive the test results back, I would arrange a conference with her and perhaps we could update her 504 Plan. I did not have a problem with her teacher. To me, she was the best fifth grade teacher at my school. She had been Allen's and Lisa's teacher. Strangely, I began to see a difference in Kim's writing. It was her own writing with fewer misspelled words and reversals. I asked Kim about this and she told me that she had help from other students. Well, that might be the only way for Kim to pass the fifth-grade.

From that meeting, I decided to take the risk and have a special pair of glasses made for Kim.

Since I already had the prescription, all I needed was to take the time and go to the optician's shop. He was very patient with Kim, as she placed different colored lenses to the light. The optician asked Kim to read the chart looking through the colored lens that she chose. The colored lense that she liked the best was a light lilac color. When she looked through that lense, she read the letters with absolutely no problems. She had always had troubled stumbling over the letters, during her many eye examinations. This was quite refreshing to see her not stumble. Along with the lense, Kim would have a stylish pair of frames and a reflective coating placed on the lenses. Since these glasses were custom-made, it would take more than a month to receive them.

A week after that, I went back to see Dr. B and the results of Kim's numerous tests. It was evident, from the results, that Kim had dyslexia, dysgraphia and an auditory-processing disorder. She was quick with her hands and could remember information.

She scored very high in certain areas and low in areas involving reading, spelling and copying.   Dr. B. had supportive information for me to go with an L.D. placement. I was very skeptical about what to do. The results were on paper in front of me.   Her juvenile glaucoma was one issue and the other disabilities were another. Dr. B. thought that Kim should receive special education for her learning disabilities and a 504 Plan for her juvenile glaucoma. Regardless, of what the results showed, I knew that Kim had a real zest for learning. I keenly remembered that when she was being fitted for her new glasses, she asked numerous questions about the lense and the reflection of light. She used adult vocabulary and seemed to understand the answers that the optician supplied. At that time, I thought Kim would make a great optician. I wanted her to have the opportunity to graduate from high school.

After looking over the results, I decided to ask Dr. B. what he thought of scotopic sensitivity and the use of colored lenses. I brought him the literature from the Internet and he looked over it. He said that if it were his child, he would try the colored lenses. Surprisingly, he stated that if the colored lenses worked, that the results of Kim's tests would be worthless.

Dr. B's paperwork for Kim would be valid in a court of law for approximately three years. So, I had time to think about, if I wanted to use it or not. Dr. B. was so taken with Kim that he offered her the opportunity to attend a private school designed for learning disabilities that he helped sponsor. The school had scholarships and Kim obviously had the opportunity to attend free. The only stipulation was that the school did not provide transportation. I recorded the information and decided to see how Kim adapted to her new glasses.

When Kim received her special glasses, she was thrilled. She was reading the billboard signs with clarity. She came up to me and said, "so that's what you look like." Apparently, Kim had never seen a clear face. When I think of it now, she did look at me strangely when growing up. She was always studying my face and placing her hands on it. She always seemed to have problems identifying me from her sitter. Both of us wore glasses and had long hair. It must have been confusing for her as a young child.

The first report card Kim received after wearing her special glasses, showed academic improvement. Kim had finally raised her grade from a 'D' in reading to a 'C'. Her teacher no longer made comments about Kim being below grade level or needing to take more time with her writing to avoid careless errors. She had a 'B' in all subjects, except a 'D' in writing. I knew that it would take time for Kim to improve in this area. She had seen everything in an abstract way in her formative years of instruction. Her only method to learn properly came from any kinesthetic methods that might have been used. How frustrating it must have been for her! Her teacher told me that she was writing smaller and more clearly. I had looked at her papers and I saw fewer errors in writing words correctly, from her various assignments. Strangely, Kim began to spot errors in other students' work and so she did not need the assistance of her friends any longer.

When I went back to the neurologist, I shared with him the information I had about scotopic sensitivity and Kim's drastic improvement. Presently, more information about scotopic sensitivity was on the Internet and how it was tied with dyslexia and ADD. He was very much impressed with my findings. Since I was there, I wanted Kim to ride the handicapped bus next school year with Allen and so I asked him to write a note. I did not feel that walking home was safe for her. I knew that she was capable, but since so many children skipped school in the local neighborhood, I did not want to risk her safety in walking to and from the bus stop. Lisa had numerous experiences with a gang of girls in the neighborhood and I had no intention of going through it again. Since, not everything can be proven, I exaggerated some about Kim's condition and so he wrote the note. He did mention that optic nerve damage was hard to analyze. Therefore, no one could really disprove Kelley's vision difficulties.

The only problem about Kim riding in a special bus, was that she could not stay back after-school. They did not arrange a late bus for handicap students. If Kim had to stay back after school, we would have to arrange to pick her up.

At the end of the fifth-grade, Kim had been one of four to make the all-city chorus ensemble from our school. Kim was on top of the world. She graduated from elementary school and became very popular from her status, as a good singer. Furthermore, we received her scores back from the required state tests and Kim had done very well. She passed most subject areas, except Social Studies and she was only a few points off.

During that summer, Kim and Lisa sang for the annual picnic held for the blind at a local park. They had a cheap karaoke machine and sung most of their songs that way. One song was done with only Lisa playing the viola and Kim singing a song from the Disney movie, 'The Little Mermaid.' They loved the girls and invited them back next year. I knew that if I had the time and could pursue it, I would have had the girls perform for more functions.

In the fall, I went to an open forum sponsored by the local newspaper on ways in which education could be improved. I wrote what I thought was a good input on what could improve education. To me, the school system needed to offer better vision screening techniques. I had written a plausible paper, but was interrupted before I could finish reading it. The person in charge, said I was making a speech. Well, it was apparent that ignorance completely consumed this audience and the reporters. Therefore, remaining ignorant contributes to the misunderstanding of vision and what kind of impact it has on how a child is going to learn. Buying new books and hiring better teachers, might make a difference, but the main impact would be to have proper vision screening for all students. The educational setting will never get better, until it is understood that more than seventy percent of what we learn, comes from what we are able to see.

I was driven to go back on the Internet and learn more about appropriate vision screening. Eventually, I became involved with Prevent Blindness and the crucial importance of their organization. They would train parents and teachers on how to screen children. There was equipment that they could borrow to assist. The only drawback was having the school system support the training. Presently, all vision screening was done by the school nurses from the Department of Public Health. I was determined that eventually I would find a way to make a difference.

Kim was excited about entering middle school and I was skeptical. I had dealt with 504 Plans with Lisa and Allen. So, what Kim experienced that year was inexcusable.

Chapter Eight

Traumatic Complications and Victory Using A 504 Plan

When all three of my children were on 504 Plans, I should have felt elated. After all, I had their medical letters of diagnosis and their 504 Plans. I made sure that I had their letters and 504 Plans updated annually. I did more than what I really had to do. A child's placement on a 504 Plan is good for three years and a medical letter of diagnosis is good for two to three years. When it came time to see if the child still qualified, which is based on a three-year term, that is when an updated medical letter of diagnosis is needed.

I kept track of all records. I felt more comfortable in updating a 504 Plan, as well as medical letters. I kept a box for each child's records and made weekly notes kept in files on my computer, in case I had to refer to any situation. It was time consuming, but in the end I would receive more respect, when having to deal with any issues that violated my children's 504 Plans.

Even though, I did my parental obligations, problems were forthcoming. Usually, it occurred with some teachers. For those, who made my children's lives miserable, they played ignorantly. I had to become an individual known as the 'B-Mom' and take action. When I knew that they were violating my children's academic rights, I approached the situation with a letter to the case manager and a copy of that particular child's 504 Plan. It was a constant battle for me, since I worked in the school system and they knew this. The likelihood of my suing was highly unlikely, unless I was willing to resign from teaching. I had a taste of that experience the year that Allen had his so-called nervous breakdown. The next day after that incident, I was observed and written up as not being a qualified teacher. The observation occurred when my class and I came back from recess. I began their math lesson, when possible. They wrote down and documented everything I did. From my experience, no one is perfect. She had a reputation of getting rid of anyone that she felt threatened her career in some way. I believed she felt threatened, because her handling of Allen's situation was liable. Then, I was worried about Allen and did not realize the potential of a lawsuit. I was placed on a plan-of-action along with several others. The next year, they were all dismissed from teaching, except me. It took three long years to get the slate clean. In doing so, I became more involved in community service, having my students receive national publication in magazines, write educational articles and try to receive any professional recognition I could obtain. Ultimately, I made the following achievements: I had more than thirty students receive national publication in a magazine, participated in nonprofit organizations, had been recognized as a writer myself and became associated with some professional organizations. The results of my endeavors placed me in a different situation. I brought prestige and recognition to my school, since no one at my school was presently involved in these affairs. It was hard and time consuming, but I had to shine. I never wanted to go through that feeling of total helplessness again.

Since all of my children had their plans and medical letters, I made sure I met at the beginning of the school year with their teachers, in hopes of insuring a prosperous year for them. When Lisa began high school, her guidance counselor became her case manager. This arrangement was great. The counselor had more access to visit Lisa's teachers when there became a problem. I was not able to meet with her teachers at the beginning of the year, except at open-house. Still, I could meet with an assistant principal, who was in charge of looking over 504 Plans. I had to only meet with him and the guidance counselor. When there became a problem with a teacher, all I had to do was call the case manager. Ms. B. was terrific! She would remain Lisa's case manager, as long as she were at that school. This gave her a chance to get to know Lisa and eventually she offered assistance in helping Lisa with any future problems. Lisa's life would never be perfect. Sometimes, a security guard hauled her down to the office for not following oral directions. Lisa learned to speak up for herself and identify that she had a handicap condition. Eventually, Lisa received the honor of being in the top 2 percent of her graduating class and was selected into Who's Who Among American High School Students. She had her picture taken in the newspaper, something my husband and I intend on eventually framing. Lisa's academic success obviously depended solely on the handling and implementation of her 504 Plan.

Just as Lisa's academic success depended on the implementation of her 504 Plan, the same holds for Allen. When Allen entered middle school, his communication skills' teacher would be his case manager. Luckily, the teachers were arranged in clusters and it was convenient for them to meet and discuss their students. Allen received preferential seating and the teachers made sure he had his homework written in his planner. Allen was allowed to print his work, since he could not do cursive. They did not time him on any tests and he was given an adaptive P.E. class. I had asked for a handicapped bus to pick him up, but my request was not granted at that time.

On the first day of school, I met with the bus driver and Allen was allowed to sit up front. The seat he sat in was the smallest seat on the bus. Presently, Allen was overweight and took up most of that seat. Unfortunately, the bus driver would put a disruptive student next to Allen. That was the only way she could drive the bus without being distracted. One day the bus driver placed a troublesome girl next to Allen. Allen had mentioned that the girl had blocked his effort on getting off the bus. The bus driver had to intervene and get onto the girl. He had told me she was always causing trouble for everyone. As usual, I always waited at the bus stop in the morning with Allen. When Allen got on the bus, the girl was already sitting in his seat. She took up most of the room and all Allen had was a small section to sit on. As I was preparing to drive away, a car pulled up. Out jumped a woman, who quickly came to my car. She had asked me if I were Allen's mother. She was upset with her daughter's treatment on the bus by the bus driver and was hoping that Allen had told me something about it. I flatly told her about her daughter's behavior toward my son. She felt that my son should give up his seat and let her daughter have it. I explained about the civil liability of having my son give up his seat.

The next morning, I spoke with the bus driver regarding the incident and that I wanted the female student removed from Allen's seat. This particular parent was closed to having harrassment charges filed, since she constantly followed behind the bus on its route. If she could do that, why not just take her daughter to school, instead. Eventually, they suspended the student off the bus.

Sometimes, Allen had trouble walking home from school. Since he walked with a gait, it took him time to cross a street and sometimes a driver would not slow down for him. So, he came close to being hit several times. One day another student had jumped him. Since Allen's reflexes were slow, he could not defend himself. If it had not been for several other students he walked home with, it is uncertain what would have happened. They had suspended this student from another school and he was roaming the streets. He was tied in with a gang that his two older brothers organized. The gang was known for threatening and terrorizing other students in the neighborhood. The next day I took off from work and went down to place a complaint against the boy. I learned that they could issue the complaint in three days, but it would take up to six months before they heard it in court. The complaint would have my name on it. Well, that was just great! Since my husband and I both worked, how could I make sure that nothing would happen to Lisa, Allen or our property, if they decided to seek vengeance. I told the advisor to forget it. It was not worth it. Instead, I pushed even more for a handicapped bus for Allen.

When I approached the school again, I met with the assistant principal. He informed me that I would have to meet with the child study team. I thought that meeting with the team was strange and I should have gone with my intuition. The team consisted of Allen's guidance counselor, the school psychologist, the nurse and the assistant. principal. During this meeting, the assistant principal was constantly being called to the office. The school psychologist was the same one involved with Allen's second screening in elementary school. I remembered that she had two children that were autistic. I was in for a rude awakening. What I thought should be a simple meeting about assigning a special bus for Allen, turned out to be another situation. I did not think about bringing any of Allen's documentation. I had to listen to written information from each of Allen's teachers, about his performance. He was doing fine and I already knew this. It was mentioned by his guidance counselor that Allen would not qualify for honors communication skills next year. Well, I told her that was fine, since that was his weakest area. I learned that Allen had passed his Algebra predictor's test and would take Algebra I next year. When the counselor finished discussing Allen's overall performance, I asked about a special bus for Allen. Mrs. F.(the psychologist) immediately interrupted and told me that I would not have this problem, if he had been placed in special education. She insisted that he was autistic. I calmly explained to Mrs. F. that they had misdiagnosed Allen and that the correct diagnosis was moderate cerebral palsy. She began to drill me about the similarities and differences of autism and cerebral palsy. I finally saw 'red' and mentioned her lack of professionalism. She was not a doctor and she could not dispute a doctor's diagnosis. She calmed herself, and so did I. Later, I learned that she was having difficulty with her own children's placement in special education.

A week later, I was helping Allen to organize his book bag and came across a paper acknowledging Allen's acceptance into their top honor's program next year. Allen would be with the top thirty students in the rising seventh-grade class. This special class would receive Algebra I and all other honor classes. At this point in Allen's life, this was a truly great opportunity. He had a dream of designing his own computer games. His ultimate goal was to become a software engineer.

Before the school year was over, I received a phone call from Allen's school. It was early in the morning and I had just arrived at work. I remember taking the call from my school's office. It was the dean letting me know that Allen had been in a bus accident. It was not serious and he just wanted me to know about the incident. All of the children were checked over by the school nurse and everyone was fine. I asked to speak with my son. Allen mumbled that he was hurting. I immediately ask the secretary at my school to arrange for a substitute. When I approached the school, I saw a police cruiser being picked up by a tow truck. Allen was in the clinic and he was complaining about his neck. The nurse told me that no one else was complaining about being injured, except Allen. I ignored her and asked for an accident report to be filled out. I had to go to the office and get it. Before I left the school, I looked for a signature. I am glad I did, because they did not sign it. I went back in and was told to return tomorrow to pick it up. I was not a fool! I had twenty-four hours to take Allen to a physician with the paperwork that would hold the school liable. I demanded that they should sign the paper immediately!

Allen's neck was sprained and he required a padded brace. He wore that brace for two weeks, before he could take it off and on. Allen had told me about the accident. The bus driver was not at fault. A police car was chasing a suspect and ran into the bus, while the bus was parked waiting to unload the students.

On the news, they described the scene as a civilian driver running into an empty bus. One of my colleagues told me to file a complaint against the police department. Maybe, I should have, but I did not.

This incident did open the door for Allen receiving a handicap bus. After all, he should have been on one in the first place. Allen did not have the necessary reflexes to protect himself when the bus was hit.

Allen had a great year in seventh-grade and that was because he had a terrific case manager. She was his communication skills' teacher and had gone through treatment for cancer. She wore special shoes, since she had difficulty walking. Maybe, that is why she was right for Allen. She knew what it felt like to be different. He was accepted into the National Junior Honor Society and felt ten feet tall. At the end of the year, Allen cried about this special teacher leaving. She would have been his case manager for next year, but she received a better position and grabbed it. Without her, Allen's eighth grade experience was something that was hard to describe by mere words.

When Allen began the eighth-grade, Kim was entering the sixth grade. So, they rode the same special bus. As usual, the information on both children was up-to-date. The school did not acknowledge my request to meet with their teachers at the beginning of the year. The school had another new principal and so I had to speak with her. When I spoke to her about requesting an informal meeting, she quickly handed the phone over to her secretary. The secretary took my name and number down and I would receive a call from the assistant principal. When he did call, he was yawning and sounded annoyed with the conversation. The dean would handle my request. They knew how to pass the buck. I knew this was going to be an interesting year!

What took place that year deserves a story all its own. The cruelty that my two children went through, led to an investigation handled by the administration of the school system.

The principal, assistant principal and dean had to do some quick household cleaning, when the sh...t hit the fan.

The investigation into how my children's 504 Plans were being handled, occurred toward the end of the school year. Before that explosion, I had tried to handle it with the dean and the assistant principal and then the principal. I went through the protocol of having something done. I wrote a letter to the dean, following my children's second reporting period.

Below is a copy of the letter:

Dear Dean H.,

I have recently looked over my children's report cards and I was appalled! These are the recommendations that I request to be made: Allen will be allowed to make up all necessary work in Honors Earth Science for the second nine weeks. Since Allen did not have a case manager intervening on his behalf, the 504 Plan was not respected. I need to see a list of these assignments by the end of next week.

As for Kim, I am requesting the following accommodations: 1. That all of her material be enlarged. 2. That she not be timed on any tests. 3. That she receive help in organizing materials from a teacher. Preferably, someone who understands Kim's disability. 4. That Kim's workload be modified. 5. That Kim be given additional time to complete her work, due to the eye fatigue that she suffers from.

Also, I am not very happy with Kim's current reading teacher. I am requesting that another reading teacher intervene and show Ms. C. how to use more appropriate teaching strategies. Kim is not a guinea pig to be practiced on. I want to see her succeeding!

If I need to meet with these teachers, then arrange a meeting directly. There needs to be consideration made in setting up a convenient time. Both of us know what lies ahead, if these issues are not addressed. Also, I realize that this is not your jurisdiction, but who does handle this?

The truth of the situation is that it has taken time and money to have my children properly diagnosed. Then, to have an appropriate 504 Plan written up and to know I don't really have to have one. The 504 Plan is really to help the teachers. According to the Department of Civil Rights, the teachers must provide an appropriate classroom instruction, since it is known that my children have a disability. So, it is an insult to the teaching profession when their 504 Plans are ignored. I already know that if it is addressed on a higher level, these teachers will be observed and a letter will be placed in their record. Therefore, I am offering them an opportunity to improve.

I grow weary of this cat and mouse game I have played this year. All I want is for my children to succeed and I don't think it is asking for more than using consideration and common sense.

I appreciate the help you can give in handling this critical situation.

*   *   *

I decided to take this letter and turn it into the school. Instead, of the secretary placing it in the dean's box, I was asked to talk with the assistant principal, instead. The dean was called to his office and we had a private conversation behind closed doors. The dean was given my letter and I was told that he would take care of it.

The following week, I received a phone call from the dean and I was asked to come in and attend two separate child study meetings for my children. I attended both meetings. I had to take a full day and prepare for a substitute for my class. The scheduled meetings were set at 12:00 p.m. and 12:30 p.m. It was not a convenient time for me and I assumed they knew this.

They told me that if I could not come, that it would take over a month to reschedule. Through my previous dealings with speaking with the dean and the assistant principal, I was hoping for results. They were sadly not following Kim's 504 Plan. Only one teacher bothered occasionally to enlarge Kim's work. They told me that it violated copyright infringement laws to enlarge her work. The dean told me this. I asked if that included the teacher-made worksheets, too. He really did not know how to answer that question. Later, I learned they were not telling me the truth. I learned from an advocacy group that they changed the law in that area and that they could enlarge any work for Kim.

As for Allen, he was failing his Earth Science class. At the beginning of the year, his case manager was his Earth Science teacher. But, the teacher was offered a better position at a university and so he took it.

I was told to write everything that I saw at home that would encompass both children. So, I took the time to do this. Both children had around two pages of notes. At this meeting, they never looked at my notes.

During Kim's meeting, a vision teacher from the special education department attended. They brought it up that Kim would not receive any vision services, unless she has an uncorrected vision acuity problem of at least 20/70. Of course, she did not have that problem. Again, I mentioned about the problem with glare. They told me that because she was on medication that it took care of the problem. I told her that it did not! Medication was needed to try to prevent any further damage. She quickly changed the subject to Dr. F.'s diagnosis, which mentioned Kim's juvenile glaucoma and optic nerve damage. Previously, before the meeting, they asked me to bring in articles and information about this disorder. I had ample info about it, but was rebuked. She had told me that his letter did not mention his diagnosis, but only referred to what I had thought. I asked her to show me what she was talking about. She could not show me and so I took out my copy and proved to her that she was wrong.

The vision teacher frankly lead the entire discussion. She asked if I wanted Kim to be referred to special education for learning disabilities and I told her 'no'. She asked what did I want. I told her I wanted the accommodations on her 504 Plan to be followed. Again, the mentioned of blowing up her work was questioned. She had mentioned that enlarging her work would be difficult. For example, what size should the letters be, since worksheets varied in font size and how much space between the words and the lines. I told her that anything was better than what she presently had.

Our discussion finally ended by an interruption by the guidance counselor. She had mentioned the time factor and that we needed to come to a decision. They quickly pointed it out that Kim did not qualify for special education and so the 504 Plan would have to be readdressed. A future meeting would be set up between her teachers and me. The vision teacher would be there, too.

The meeting closed concerning Kim and the team was ready for Allen. There were several teacher reports to confirm that he was making academic success in the classroom, except his Earth Science teacher. She had written a letter stating that he was failing because of his lab work. Her intervention was to keep the lab reports for Allen and have him finish them in the future. Well, we had run out of time, because everyone wanted to eat their lunch. They rudely got up and left. Then, I did not think about questioning how the Earth Science teacher was conducting the lab assignments. Apparently, she never intervened with Allen's consistent struggling of using the lab equipment. Everyone did their lab assignments by themselves. The appropriate way of gaining knowledge from lab work, would be to have the students work in small cooperative groups or work with a partner. The idea of working by oneself was ludicrous.

The teacher could easily have devised this type of plan and Allen would have been successful.

On March 3, 2000, I had not heard of any meeting, yet. After talking with my children, I learned more disparaging news. Kim was failing math because of being tested with an overhead. She had tried raising her hand in the past, but was usually ignored or the teacher would reply, "I will get back with you," when she could not see what was on the overhead. Therefore, she failed the tests and would continue to fail the tests. She had enlightened me about the class arrangements. She sat with the side of her face to the window. Therefore, the glare would be a constant problem for her. Her back should have been to the window. Kim's failure in her academics was clearly not of her intellect, but due to her teachers' failure to follow a 504 Plan. Kim had to deal with worksheets and books that had 12pt font or smaller, glare from overheads, being timed on tests, not being allowed to take a break for eye fatigued, not being acknowledged when she raised her hand and being intimated when handed a sheet and having to answer very quickly to the question, "Here, can you see this?" Kim's delayed reply would be, "Yes, but… only a little."

Kim's problem was enough to deal with, but I also had one with Allen. Allen was still failing his science lab, because he could not feel the textures of the various rocks, and not being able to properly to use the equipment. He was late for lunch, whenever he had Earth Science. She simply would not allow him to leave a little early. Since Allen walked with a gait and it was on his 504 Plan, it was another accommodation that she did not allow.

Upon learning all of this disheartening news, I sent a letter with some of documentation to the principal. Later, I would receive a phone call from the dean to schedule a meeting with Kim's teachers. I naively assumed that someone would look into the situation about Allen.

Earlier that week, I went back to see Kim's eye doctor and brought a list of items to be discussed. He took the time to listen, as Kim spoke up and told him what was going on. He was very concerned about the complete lack of respect for Kim's condition. In fact, the belief that treating glaucoma with medication takes care of the problem is only a myth. She would always have difficulty with glare. He took my copies of information on scotopic sensitivity, when he had heard that Harvard University accepts that condition as a learning disability. He agreed to write another more clear, precise letter.

I waited nervously to hear about the results of my letter to Kim and Allen's principal. I prayed that it did not come back to haunt me. Since I taught in the same school system, anything could happen.

Below is a copy of the letter I wrote to the school principal:

March 3, 2000

Dear _____,

I have gone through the general protocol for both of my children. Allen and Kim ————— are on 504 Plans. Since I have two children with different disabilities, I will address them one at a time.

Allen's 504 Plan was handled respectfully through Mr. T's efforts. Since he has left, Allen's needs were not handled. Attached are letters and documents that should give you a clear view of what he has been through. Recently, I went to a child study meeting for Allen, which was a complete waste of my time. Although, he has been given another case manager, I haven't seen the necessary changes in his Earth Science class. Please take time to read the attached materials.

Now, concerning my daughter, is a whole different situation. As with Allen, I recently went to a child study meeting, being persuaded into thinking that she might receive a small part of special educational services. I do not have her documentation, because her medical doctor is readdressing her disability with another letter of diagnosis and has need of the information I have. When I receive this important letter, I will send a copy to you. It was stated at the recent child study meeting that Kim's juvenile glaucoma was taken care of by medication. Her medication is used to control any further damage done to her optic nerve. It is a known fact that children with juvenile glaucoma have a problem with indoor and outdoor glare and what they tend to visualize fluctuates during the day. A copy of her 504 Plan is in her records and I would like to clarify that nothing has been followed. Recently, Kim told me that her back is not to outdoor glare, due to the class arrangements. When she raises her hand to let her teacher know that she can't see, she is either ignored or 'I'll get back with you.' But, no one ever does. She is being timed in certain classrooms. When an overhead is used, Kim can't see the paper, she tried to explain that she can only see a little bit. It is unfortunate that Kim can not receive services from the visually handicap, because she doesn't qualify with the label of 20/70 uncorrected acuity. There are some measures that could be taken, with borrowing equipment associated with the blind, but that will need to be addressed by the school and who is going to do it?

I have been very disheartened this year. Through my understanding, there has only been one teacher that has tried to assist her and understand her needs. Therefore, my daughter is failing most of her classes, due to the lack of respecting her civil rights.

I waited for three weeks. I wanted to verify, before sending a letter to the school administration office, that nothing was being done. I wrote a strong letter documenting some crucial steps that took place to try to emphasize my children's civil rights. Below is the letter:

March 30, 2000

To Whom It May Concern:

I am a very concerned parent distressed over the education of my children. Allen and Kim are receiving at ————————— ———— School. It became apparent to me at the very end of the first semester, that my children's 504 Plans were not being followed. My son, Allen, has moderate cerebral palsy. When I had learned that Allen had a replacement teacher for Earth Science and was beginning to falter in his academic growth, I approached the school. I spoke with the assistant principal and the dean. They looked into the matter and found out that he had failed his lab work. (Unfortunately, they didn't look hard enough.) I was informed that Ms. R (Earth Science teacher) was very much aware of his 504 Plan. Allen was brought back up to the child study team to see if he could qualify for services for motor impairment. Instead, he had been officially signed a new case manager (his previous Earth Science teacher had been his case manager). Ms. O (case manager) would speak with Ms. R about Allen's handicapped condition. On that same day, I met with the child study team concerning Kim. I wanted to know if she would qualify for vision services, since her 504 Plan was not being handled appropriately. It was decided by most of the team, that Kim's 504 Plan should be enforced. Later, I learned that both meetings did not change the situation for either child. Therefore, I wrote a letter to the principal describing my concerns.

Allen, who is a very bright child, is currently failing Earth Science. Allen does not have complete use of his hands and can not feel the texture of materials and would have difficulty with holding lab tools, etc. I assumed that since his letter of diagnosis from Dr. F was very explicit, anyone with common sense would have a peer work with him. Instead, I find out that Allen had to do the work by himself. Traditionally, all lab work is done in a group or pairs. Eventually, Ms. R had Allen stay after-school for completion of one lab. I naively thought that she would provide some assistance. I can't imagine anyone being that insensitive to a handicapped individual. I would like to emphasize that the use of my son's planner is non-existent. He has been forced to copy from the board. He has not been allowed to leave a few minutes early for lunch. When he has spoken up, her reply has been, 'You need to be more responsible, that's not my job.' At that time, I considered writing to you, but I put the thought on hold when I learned that she had asked Allen to stay after-school on Tuesday afternoons. This was an inconvenience for my husband, since Allen rides the handicapped bus and needed someone to pick him up. Anyway, I thought someone had intervened and knew that Allen's rights were being violated. Well, I was wrong! She saw him only once, which was on March 21st. On Tuesday, March 28th, she informed Allen that he would not be staying after school. I received my first phone message from her on the same day that the third nine weeks report card went home. Allen was told that he would need to be placed in a general science class. Unfortunately, this will alter things for my son. I do not want him to uproot his schedule, just because someone refused to teach him, due to his handicap. I feel that Allen should be allowed to redo all necessary work and that arrangements for this should at the expense of the school. Such as, a late handicapped bus bringing him home. Allen should be allowed to take the SOL test in Earth Science in May and have this test initiated by a different teacher. Allen has completed his SRI, but I would prefer to have someone else grade it. So, I will keep it, until I hear from you.

Earlier I had mentioned my daughter, Kim. Kim has juvenile glaucoma and her 504 Plan was available at the beginning of the school year. I would like to mention that it took until March, before her first worksheet was enlarged. Recently, some changes have occurred, but only the bare minimum. I had really wanted Kim to receive vision services, but was denied. I recently learned that the State Department of Education recognizes juvenile glaucoma as a degenerative eye disease and this disease qualifies her for vision services through special education. When I attended the child study meeting, the acknowledgement was not declared. When I went recently to a follow-up meeting for her 504 Plan, her vision needs were not going to be met and I was being forced to consider LD services. Two days later, I received a phone call from the dean. He had told me that he had made arrangements for Kim's work to be enlarged. At that time, he needed me to come back in to officially assign Ms. O as the case manager for Allen. I told him that I didn't feel it was necessary, since she had already been assigned at the child study meeting. But, that I would need to update his 504 Plan for next year. I told him that I needed another letter from Dr. F to state Allen's disability with climbing stairs. At that time, Allen's scheduled appointment was for March 29th. It has been changed to April 20th, due to an emergency that Dr. F had.

Attached are copies of my children's letters of diagnosis, their 504 Plans and their report cards. At the time of this writing, I don't have Kim's latest report card. I would like to express that I have all necessary correspondence documented and will send it to you, if necessary.

Another concern of mine is about next year. Since this year was awful, what do I expect for next year? Allen will probably not attend ———————— High School, since there is not an elevator. Allen would need to take an adaptive P.E. class or be excused from P.E. He would work best in a cluster team, so that his 504 Plan would be followed and that his letter of diagnosis would be read and understood. It is very uncertain about his academic placement next year, due to the Earth Science problem.

As for my daughter, Kim, she needs enlarged material and can not handle glare.

All of these issues create a huge concern. I hope that you can provide assistance in helping my two children meet their academic goals.

_____

_____

_____

My letter did receive a response. One day, unexpectantly, when I was bringing my class back from having their individual pictures taken, a tall gentleman in a business suit came up to me. He wanted to know where he could find Mrs. —————. Looking directly at him, I acknowledged who I was. I have learned from this business experience, to look directly at someone and then shake their hand. It is always important to look, as though you can handle any situation that comes up. His name was Mr. V. and he was from the administrative office. He had a copy of my letter and wanted to address the issues about which I wrote. Feeling a bit annoyed, since my class was with me, I decided to handle this intervention as quickly as possible. Mr. V. was very attentive and I thought for once that my children's problems would be eliminated.

I was right about Mr. V. Allen passed Earth Science and made the top score on the state exam. Allen's high school teachers were carefully selected. Kim's teachers would be hand-picked for the following year, too. I should be satisfied with these results and I am.

Chapter Nine

Hidden Disabilities and How to Obtain a 504 Plan

Since I am the mother of three special needs children and a classroom teacher, I understand the various techniques used in appropriate classroom management. They must address several important issues before they will grant a 504 Plan. The first is that your child must have a legitimate hidden disability. Becoming a hidden disability detective to uncover it, is important. Ask yourself the following questions: Does my child have trouble finishing classroom assignments? Completing homework? Daydreams? Fail timed tests? Writing is messy? Reads below grade level? Becomes easily eye fatigued? Have difficulty spelling words? Does the wrong assignment? Is disorganized? Can't read for long periods? Appears to have a short-attention span? If your child has any of these problems, start writing them down. The more problems your child has, the better the chance of your child having a hidden disability. Save samples of your child's work, and any notes the teacher may have written, notes took from teachers' conferences along with progress reports and report cards. Proving to a medical doctor that your child has a problem, can be time-consuming.

When going through protocol with doctors, my advice is to begin with your child's pediatrician. Remaining persistent is imperative, to get results. Definitely, have your child examined by a private eye-care professional, and an audiologist. The business with using an eye chart is bogus. Make sure to go back annually. Don't be skeptical in seeing a neurologist, even if your pediatrician is not supportive.

Enrich your knowledge on hidden disabilities, such as a central auditory processing disorder and scotopic sensitivity. These two disorders have an effect of being misrepresented in a medical diagnosis. For example, a child might appear to have an attention deficit disorder, when in fact, that child might have one of the disorders mentioned.

Don't rule out the possibility of a brain injury. Your child could have suffered from a fall or had been shaken. Brain injuries do not necessarily show results at the very beginning of injury, nor does your child have to be unconscious. Your child can show having difficulties later.

Once when it is known a disability exist, find out all there is about that disorder. To pursue a 504 Plan, all the necessary research needs to be done. It is a great time we live in, with the availability of the Internet for getting information. More than likely, to have a successful 504 Plan written, make sure that they discuss all avenues of your child's learning. Such as, modifying school work and homework. Should they time your child on tests? Will it take longer for your child to walk from one class to another? Is there a problem with your child taking P.E.? Would your child benefit from sitting up front? Should the teacher write down the homework? Is it really necessary for your child to have to copy from the board? Should they assign your child a helper? If problems exist with the regular bus, see if they can provide a handicap bus. Remember that knowledge is power!

Making copies of all documents is imperative. When approaching the school for a 504 Plan, make sure to get back either the original document or a copy. Do not leave the school without it!

Still unsure about what a 504-Plan entails or have additional questions, call or write to the Department of Civil Rights. I have included addresses of vital information in the back of this book.

Once when a 504 Plan is put into place, filing a complaint with the Department of Civil Rights is simple, if documentation can be provided. They are quick in sending the required forms to fill out. I could have over the years filed one. The only reason is that I work in the system.

Chapter Ten

A Summary of the Important Events and Strategies Customed-Designed With Each of My Children in Mind

I have learned so much being an advocate for my children's 504 Plans. Over the years, I have looked back over where they began and where they plan to go. I always wonder if I could have done more. Perhaps, if I have been more informative and knew what I know now.

In summary, my oldest child could not follow more than one direction at a time. In first grade, she did better sitting up front near the teacher, than in the back of the room. Her seating arrangement made a difference between passing and failing. As she became older, she would seldom complete her required homework if orally given. She did the same thing, concerning class work. I thought she had a hearing problem, because she would misunderstand conversation with her peers, and with her family members. I had the school give her a hearing test and later I went for private testing. No matter how often I had her tested, she always passed her tests. It was not until she began middle school that I found out about CAPD (central auditory processing disorder). Again, I took her to a private audiologist, because Lisa claimed she could not hear the sound from videos being used in the classroom. She had difficulty using the school's info-line to find out what her homework assignments were. They primarily gave her homework assignments orally in class and she used the info-line to check over what she had written. Naturally, if they orally gave specific details for the assignments, she would have problems with properly following through with these instructions. I would usually have to intervene by calling the info-line myself to verify her assignments.   At one time, a teacher criticized Lisa for continually watching her, as she walked around the room. Lisa was easily picked on by her peers, because they thought she was conceited. They claimed that she was antisocial for she rarely responded to informal greetings.   When I went to see the audiologist, I had written everything I could think of that related to a hearing disorder. The audiologist listened intently and made two suggestions. Lisa was either ADD or had CAPD. I arranged to have the test done.   The results of her three hour testing revealed that she had CAPD.   This disorder relates to the auditory nerve and that it can not properly filter sound to the brain.   Therefore, whenever background noise was evident and someone was speaking, she would not be able to properly to hear all of the information. CAPD is categorized by mild, moderate and severe. They diagnosed Lisa's disorder as mild. I naively thought that if I brought this new information about my daughter to the attention of her school that she would receive special consideration. I met with the school's child study team. The team included a psychologist, diagnostician, social worker and the assistant principal.   They designed a special IEP for her. They made suggestions, such as preferential seating, writing her homework on the board and checking her for understanding. The audiologist recommended it, who gave Lisa the test, that she should wear a FM monitor. They flatly rebuked the idea of her teachers wearing a microphone, while Lisa wore the monitor to help with filtering speech. Later, I learned that I could have pushed the issue. This so-called IEP never went into effect. There was no such thing. It was a poor substitute for a 504 Plan. During that summer, I learned about the existence of a 504 Plan from a principal. I wrote to the Department of Civil Rights and told them about my daughter's disability. I received a phone call from one consultant and learned that having suggested classroom strategies included in the diagnosis from a medical doctor was important.   The more that was included in the doctor's cover letter, the more bargaining power I had. My next move was to obtain a second opinion and have those suggestive teaching strategies implemented in the diagnosis. One cannot expect a medical doctor to write these suggested strategies in a letter of diagnosis, because a doctor is not an educator. Going on the Internet and find out about CAPD was easy. I listed my complaints and the problems Lisa was having in school and then I wrote down the teaching strategies that they could implement in the classroom. I went to a reputed otolaryngologist and showed him the evaluation of Lisa's CAPD, along with my suggested teaching strategies. The doctor evaluated Lisa and wrote a letter of diagnosis with some of my suggested teaching strategies. Now, I was in business. In the school district I taught at, a parent can request a child study meeting for his/her child. Simply request it by asking the assistant principal or principal for one. A form will need to be filled out. In middle school, they required each teacher to have written documentation on the child in questioned, if the school year had already begun. In Lisa's situation, their reports showed adequate progress. If I had only went with the audiologist's report, I probably would not have received a 504 Plan. However, since I had a diagnosis from a medical doctor along with suggested teaching strategies, they could not deny me. Her 504 Plan was written up and signed by everyone present. Her classroom teachers did not have to sign the plan, but must be made aware of it. A 504 Plan is only legitimate, if they truly write it on a 504 form. The words '504 Plan' will be written at the top of it. I have included a copy of her first 504 Plan, and the medical doctor's letter in this book. To insure that this 504 Plan is carried out and protects Lisa's rights, they assign a case manager. This person can be a classroom teacher, counselor or even the principal. Realistically, it should be someone who is familiar with the child's disability. If there are problems with the implementation of the plan, the parent can write a note to the case manager. He or she would discuss the matter over with the person in question. If I were not comfortable with the results, I could get in touch with the principal and request a meeting to resolve the violation of my child's civil rights. Whenever, any disputable situation occurred, most of the time, they handled it quickly. If it had not been, a letter to the superintendent would be forthcoming. If your child's civil rights have been violated and written proof is available, contact the Department of Civil Rights and include a copy of your child's 504 Plan, along with the medical diagnosis. At the end of this book are regional addresses. They will send a letter with forms to fill out, after they are contacted. Also, they can be reached online and information can be entered through that method. Perhaps, a situation that would call for that extreme measure will never come up. To insure that Lisa's 504 Plan remains strong, I take her back for a yearly checkup and have her medical doctor write an updated letter. Usually, this needs to be done every two years. I have heard in certain situations, it can updated every three years, because that's when the 504 Plan is re-evaluated. It's important to find out for sure, because each school district might be a bit different in that perspective. It is critical that you file all important papers. Never allow the school system to keep the original of your doctor's evaluation. You keep it and have them make a copy. Don't leave the meeting without a copy of the 504 Plan in your hand, too. Even if certain individuals forgot to sign it, they can send you another copy of it (completely signed) in the mail. You never know what will happen to your documents and if they will be securely kept in your child's cumulative record. I have had problems in the past, when certain forms were not in my child's cumulative folder and I had to have the school make copies of my originals.

Lisa has been on a 504 Plan for over five years. Her GPA is above a 3.5 and it looks as though she has a chance for college. After Lisa received her 504 Plan, I had to go through the same ordeal again with my son. Unfortunately, my son had been misdiagnosed earlier and this did cause some problems. It was first determined in the primary grades, that he had autism/ADD, because he tended to daydream, had communication problems, and poor gross and fine motor skill problems. In other words, he couldn't skip, run fast, write legibly, had difficulty copying assignments from the board, he would fail at timed tests and would become a behavioral problem due to stress-related activities. He was referred to the child study team by the principal. I had to put up a fight to keep him from qualifying in a special educational program for emotionally-disturbed children. It was like placing a round peg into a square hole. It was obvious there was something wrong with Allen, but my motherly instinct guided me into not allowing a wrong placement for my son. I knew that he was brain-damaged, but it didn't come from birth. It either came from a car accident that occurred when he was two years old and he had hit the back of his head (but was not unconscious) or it came from being roughly shakened in a pre-school (I did not find this out until later). Allen was seeing a psychologist that I was not happy with. Allen had stated that he felt he was living in someone else's body. Allen's way of expressing himself was not actually being understood by the psychologist and others. I became paranoid every time Allen opened his mouth. Later, I took Allen to a neurologist. I wrote the problems Allen was having in school. Through more extensive tests, I learned that Allen had a mild form of cerebral palsy. This new diagnosis along with suggested teaching strategies, opened the door for a 504 Plan. Some of the teaching strategies came from suggestions given for ADD students. Allen could have qualified for a 504 Plan for having dysgraphia, or mini-seizures (which resembles daydreaming). Dysgraphia encumbers the student from taking timed tests and copying from the board. The amount of class work and homework would have to be modified.

In the back of this book, you will find an address where you can obtain information about ADD and the suggested teaching strategies used for students with that disability. These suggestions are flexible and can be used with other hidden disabilities.

I had thought that keeping up with two 504 Plans, along with being an advocate was all I could reasonably handle. Well, I had to learn to handle one more.

My youngest child, Kim, had difficulty when she began kindergarten. I had thought she was a bit slow. She seemed to have trouble learning letters and their sounds. She entered first-grade and easily fell behind the other students. She went for reading remediation, but ended up repeating first-grade. Kim had always complained about not seeing the board. She would claim that something was blocking her vision. I had totally misunderstood her meaning. I thought she meant that someone was sitting in front of her and she couldn't see the board. She was periodically checked by the school nurse for her vision. Eventually, I learned that reading an eye chart would not identify her problem. I took her to an ophthalmologist and he thought she was immature. He wanted to recheck her in two years, She only had a slight near-sighted problem and it did not require glasses. Kim seemed to show improvement, as she repeated first-grade. I seldom saw reversals in her writing and she wrote legibly and neatly on her paper. When she entered second-grade, the problems seem to come back. Her writing was messy and she was just barely handling on-grade level work. I thought she was being lazy and I blamed it on the teacher. When Kim entered the third-grade, I knew she would have a rough time. Her writing was atrocious and she would skip small words in her reading. She had a tracking problem and easily lost her place when reading. I took her to a reputable optometrist, who was popular in the area of vision therapy. I felt that Kim had dyslexia with a tracking problem. She went for vision therapy for six months. I saw some change, but not as much as I had expected. Kim was staying after-school for remediation in reading for an hour and a half each school day. It was a very difficult time for her. She was still required to do her homework in the evening. During one of the optometrist's vision screenings for Kim, he noticed her eye pressure was high and he wanted a second opinion. What was strange about Kim's eye pressure, was that it was not consistent. Reluctantly, I went back to the same ophthalmologist Kim saw when she was in first-grade. Kim was checked from a total of five visits, before it was determined that she had juvenile glaucoma. Kim was now wearing glasses and taking eye medication. I thought this was the answer to her problems in reading and writing. Since she had a disability, I pursued a 504 Plan for her. Her ophthalmologist was very reluctant with writing educational strategies in his diagnosis. He assumed that the school system would be willing to help my daughter with providing educational assistance. I had to be aggressive and secure a handbook written by the Glaucoma Research Foundation. Their address is found at the end of this book. Her doctor used some of these suggestions in his cover letter. Kim would be given breaks to rest her eyes, she would not be timed on her tests, she would have preferential seating to avoid glare and be allowed to use bold-contrast print. Even though, I had secured a 504 Plan for Kim, I was not satisfied. Kim was making it on her own, without remedial reading. Her grades varied. She could make high grades, and then all of a sudden make low grades. At least, she could make high grades and I felt her 504 Plan was helping with that. Occasionally, Kim complained of not seeing the board. In fact, she described something white covering the board. At home, Kim sat directly in front of our big screen television. She claimed that if she sat away from it, the faces were distorted. Kim began to tell me other strange occurrences. She told me that words would run off the page when she read. She still omitted small words when she was reading. She wrote large on her paper, because she couldn't see her writing. This was so strange to me. She was wearing her glasses and taking eye medication for her glaucoma. What more could I do for her? I took her back to her eye doctor and he told me that her pressure was fine. But, one thing that always annoyed me was why she could never read the doctor's eye chart without making a mistake. She always made mistakes. She told her doctor that she saw dots and told him about her other problems. He thought she was psychosomatic.

I ended up taking Kim to my son's neurologist. I thought perhaps there was a problem with her optic nerve. He was concerned about her writing, but the rest he thought was psychosomatic. He made arrangements to have her tested by a neuropsychologist. Before this occurred, Lisa had lost her glasses and needed a new pair. I went to our regular optician to purchase another pair of glasses. While I was there, I saw a display of colored lens. I asked the optician about them. He told me that colored lens help some people with glare, primarily fluorescent lighting. I didn't think much more about it, until one day I was net surfing. I came upon an article about scotopic sensitivity. This disability relates to how the optic nerve filters light. It can create symptoms of dyslexia and make copying from the board and writing on paper difficult. A person with scotopic sensitivity would have a problem with glare coming from flourescent lighting. Kim's classroom had this kind of lighting, which most schools do. I took this information with me and had Kim's neuropsychologist look over it. He told me it was possible that this disorder does exist. From his testing, Kim had dyslexia and a dysgraphia problem. He recommended special education. But, I wanted to be an advocate in Kim's education. I felt uncomfortable with the choice of special education, because I didn't see how this program would help her. The treatment of scotopic sensitivity is done by wearing certain colored filter lenses. The information about this disability, as well as the suggested treatment is listed in the back of this book. There was not anyone qualified to treat this disorder and so I used my own instinct in finding a way to help Kim. I knew of a master optician, who specialized in colored lens with a reflective glare coating. Kim spent over an hour experimenting with the lenses and finally selecting light, lilac colored lenses. Once when she looked through one of them, she read the letters on the chart with no errors. She read the chart quickly, too. It was uncanny! Kim had never read an eye chart like that! In fact, Kim soon learned that she had never truly seen anything clearly before in her life, until she looked through those lenses. Her neuropsychologist told me that her tests would be considered invalid, if these colored lenses did the trick.

I decided to continue with Kim's 504 Plan, since she would have eye fatigue due to her eye medication. When I upgrade her 504 Plan, I will include her work being modified, in regards to her eye fatigue.

If a child is on medication, due to a disability, it would be beneficial to see about a 504 Plan, when the use of medication can hinder the child's academic performance and productivity.

Be sure to look over the addresses of information I have provided at the end of this book.

Appendix

If you write to this general address, they will send you a listing of the regional addresses:

> U.S. Department of Education
> Office for Civil Rights
> 330 C. Street, S.W. 5th Floor
> Washington, D.C. 20202

*If you write to this address, ask for the following publications:

"The Guidance Counselor's Role in Ensuring Equal Educational Opportunity."

"The Civil Rights of Students with Hidden Disabilities Under Section 504 of the Rehabilitation Act
of 1973."

"Placement of School Children with Aids."

"Discipline of Students with Handicaps in Elementary and Secondary Schools."

"Free Appropriate Public Education for Students with Handicaps."

"The Rights of Individuals with Handicaps Under Federal Law."

"Students Placement in Elementary and Secondary Schools and Section 504."

"Auxiliary Aids and Services for Postsecondary Students with Handicaps."

Information for ADD/ADHD

A great resource for classroom strategies can be found on the internet. Go to a search engine, such as webcrawler and type out the words for the entire disability. I found this particular website to be helpful: www.Ldonline.org

*When you reach this site, you will see the search box on the right. Simply enter 'ADHD' and you will find plenty of information.

Information for CAPD (Central Auditory Processing Disorder)

Write to this organization and request information on CAPD:

> NIDCD Information Clearinghouse
> 1 Communication Avenue
> Bethesda, MD 20892-3456
> Website: www.nidcd.nih.gov

(NIDCD = National Institute on Deafness and Other Communication Disorders Information Clearinghouse)

Other organizations that can provide information:

National Parent Information Network
website: www.npin.org

Learning Disabilities Association of America
website: www.Ldanatl.org

National Information Center on Children and Youth with Disabilities (NICHCY)
website: www.nichcy.org

For Vision-Related Problems:

Concerning juvenile glaucoma, you can download a copy of this reference guide from the Glaucoma Research Foundation.

website: www.glaucoma.org

for the reference guide: www.glaucoma.org/glaucoma.html (You will see a list of free resources. Click on the entry that states 'childhood glaucoma.'

Another organization that may offer free information about vision disorders is the International Dyslexia Association.

DISCLAIMER: The information I have provided in this book comes from my own experience. The names and places were changed, but the events actually took place. My book is written for informational purposes and serves only in that capacity and no other.

(412) 341-1515 - ask for your local chapter

National Information Center on Children and Youth with Disabilities (NICHCY) 1-800-695-0285

For Vision-Related Problems:

concerning juvenile glaucoma write to this organization and request a copy of this reference guide:

"Childhood Glaucoma: A Reference Guide for Families:

> Glaucoma Research Foundation
> 490 Post Street
> Suite 830
> San Francisco, CA 94102

To find information about scotopic sensitivity (also known as Irlen Syndrome) go to the internet and use any general search engine. You can try to use this web address: http://student.ecok.edu/admdept/studserv/sssirlin2.html

Other sources to look up on the internet are:

> The International Dyslexia Association
> Dyslexia 2000 Network
> Mental Health Net
> The Association for Comprehensive Neurotherapy

DISCLAIMER: The information I have provided in this book comes from personal experience. The names and places were changed, but the events actually took place. My book is written for informational purposes and serves only in that capacity and no other.

Samples of Children's Medical Letters and 504 Plans

Sahron Ollie

MEDICAL SCHOOL
DEPARTMENT OF OTOLARYNGOLOGY – HEAD AND NECK SURGERY

July 13, 1995

Re:
Record #: 3874D
Office visit: 7/13/95

Dear Mrs.

Thank you for the opportunity to see Lisa. in th
office on 7/13/95. As we discussed, it does appea
that Lisa's previous extensive evaluation i
consistent with a diagnosis of central auditor
processing disorder. This implies that while th
peripheral auditory apparatus is intact, there i
difficulty with integration of auditory informatic
to allow for complete comprehension. As you ar
aware, this is a very difficult disorder to treat
and it is imperative that nonauditory clues b
enhanced to substitute for the lack of auditor
comprehension.

My recommendations include preferential seating i
the classroom to maximize the clarity of th
teacher's speech. Lisa should be seated away fro
potential conflicting noise sources such a
hallways or playground noise. Auditory signal
should be enhanced by use of appropriate facia
expressions, hand gestures, and body language.
FM auditory trainer system or other individua
listening device is highly recommended to maintai
constant alertness of the teacher and child.
would likely benefit from a reduced delivery of th
speech message to allow for the delay in centra
integration. Finally a speech and languag
evaluation with emphasis on receptive languag
abilities is necessary.

I hope that my recommendations have been of som
comfort to you, and I am optimistic that with a
individual educational plan Lisa will continue t
excel in school and social interaction.

§504 Plan
(Educational Plan for Assuring Equal Access under Section 504)

Name Lisa		DOB	Date 2-3-97
Student Number / /	School Middle	Grade 8	CA 14

The following accommodations/services are considered necessary for the above named student as a result of his/her qualification as handicapped under §504.

- use of buddy system to be sure Lisa can check homework and instructions
- seat Lisa closest to where the teacher gives the most auditory instructions
- obtain Lisa's attention before giving instructions
- use visual cues & aids whenever possible
- give time to verbally respond to auditory instruction
- ask short questions
- have Lisa watch the mouths of teachers as they speak
- assist in organizing verbal responses
- use of daily planner (Lisa)
- assist Lisa to develop organizational skills

§504 Plan Case Manager:

§504 Plan Participants and Date:

2/3/97
2/3/97
2-3-97
G.P. 2/4/97

White: School Student Folder (Cat. II)   Yellow: Case Manager   Pink: Parent   B-36

93

Sahron Ollie

CHILD AND ADOLESCENT NEUROLOGY
NEURO-DEVELOPMENTAL CENTER

TELEPHONE
FACSIMILE

June 22, 1999

OFFICE NOTE

RE: Allen
DOB: 4/11/85
MR#:

Allen is a 14-year-old with severe graphomotor disability, gross and fine motor incoordination, enuresis and sleep problems. His incoordination has been attributed to a prenatally acquired cerebellar abnormality (cerebral palsy) and is a major issue which prevents him from adequately participating in many activities. He is unable to perform legible cursive writing, to use silverware properly, to tie his shoes, to sort and manage his school papers, or to walk with a normal gait. These processes are improving with age and therapy but by no means are they resolved.

As noted in the past, his work load needs to be modified. Tests should be given on an untimed basis. He should be allowed adequate time to complete work whenever necessary. He has a great deal of difficulty copying from the board and should be provided copies of either a classmate's or teacher's notes. His tendency to daydream is a reaction to school stressors and will usually respond to stress reduction efforts. Headaches follow a similar pattern. Homework assignments should be completable within a reasonable time frame based on observation of his school work habits.

For the record, he weighed 86 kg., was 168 cm. tall, had a blood pressure of 120/63, pulse was 91, FOC was 58.5 cm.

57

§504 Plan

(Educational Plan for Assuring Equal Access under Section 504)

Name Allen		DOB 4-11-85	Date 5-6-97
Student Number	School		Grade 5	CA

The following accommodations/services are considered necessary for the above named student as a result of his/her qualification as handicapped under §504.

The following accomodations are recommended for Allen :

1) Modify work and allow extra time for written assignments.

2) Standardized testing will be given with extra time allotted.

3) Word processing will be provided for writing assignments.

4. Allen may need a keylock for his locker as he is unable to manipulate a combination lock.

5) Parents will provide organizational materials to specifically address each class (ie. accordion folder, pocket folders.

6) Modifications will be needed in physical education to deal with fine and gross motor limitations.

§504 Plan Case Manager: _____

§504 Plan Participants and Date:

White: School/Student Folder (Cat. II)   Yellow: Case Manager   Pink: Parent   B-36

Sahron Ollie

SCHOOL

September 7, 1999

MEMORANDUM

TO: Mrs. ████
           Mrs. ████
           Mr. ███
           Mrs. ███
           Mr. ████
           Mrs. ████
           Mr. █████

FROM: ███████, Dean of Students

RE: Educational Plan Under Section 504 for Kim ██████

CC: Mrs. ██████, Parent
           Mrs ██████, Guidance Counselor

The following accommodations/services are considered necessary for the above named student as a result of her qualification as handicapped under *S* 504.

1)   *Large print materials (black on white) will be available if necessary.*
2)   *Educational materials presented against a simple background. Keep work area uncluttered.*
3)   *Use high contrast (dark colors against white background) and bold writing in materials.*
4)   *Shorten assignments to avoid fatigue.   (Long reading passages or copy work).*
5)   *Preferential seating with her back to the window to reduce glare.*
6)   *Kim will let the teacher know if her eyes are fatigued.*
7)   *Built in break if needed.*
8)   *Break up testing over a long period of time.*

If you have any questions, please see me or call ████████████████████.
Elementary at ██████

Children's Specialty Group, PLLC
CHILD AND ADOLESCENT NEUROLOGY
Neuro-Developmental Center

Telephone
Fax

April 20, 2000

RE: Kim
DOB: 8/21/87
MR#:

To Whom It May Concern:

Kim is a 12-year-old followed by this office for her juvenile glaucoma and scotopic sensitivity. She does have visual field losses attributable to these lesions. In addition, she has poor visual acuity that often necessitates the use of large print materials. Unfortunately, there is some inconsistency in her visual experience so that at times she may be able to use smaller print material but can not always be expected to do so.

Until Kim proves that she is safe crossing the street and walking from the bus stop to home, she should remain on a handicapped bus. Mother reports frequent incidents in which Kim appears not to see oncoming traffic.

Respectfully submitted,

DOS 4/20/00
DOT 4/24/00

Sahron Ollie

EYE PHYSICIAN AND SURGEON

TELEPHONE

March 10, 2000

Re: Kim ▮▮▮▮
DOB: 08-21-1987
Date of Visit: 02-29-00

Dear Mrs.▮▮▮▮

It was good to see Kim again for her follow-up visit concerning her Juvenile Glaucoma. The Visual Field exam, which was done on this visit, is showing some areas of superior field loss especially in the right eye. There is a small defect noted in the inferior left field as well, but this is still within normal limits. As we discussed, intra-ocular pressure was still at a good level although she had been off her Timoptic drops for several days. This would not be unusual as often times it will take a long time for the pressure to rise once a patient has been on the medication for a while. However, it will go back up so she does need to continue the drop once a day.

I was concerned to learn that Kim is still having trouble with her school work and that she is still not being given the accommodations and services that were granted to her under her Section 504 Plan. Specifically these were:
1. Large print materials (black on white) are to be available as she finds it necessary.
2. Educational materials are to be presented on simple backgrounds.
3. Written materials are to use high contrast and bold writing.
4. Assignments and testing are to be shortened by breaks to avoid fatigue.
5. Glare is to be reduced by having preferential seating with her back to the source of light.
6. Kim is to let the teacher know if her eyes are too fatigued to work.

In addition to these measures, I would suggest that overhead projector materials should be large and in very high contrast. This would be a corollary to numbers 1 and 3 above.

Sincerely,

www.ingramcontent.com/pod-product-compliance
Lightning Source LLC
Chambersburg PA
CBHW030351290526
45785CB00004B/1703